GAUGUIN'S
INTIMATE JOURNALS

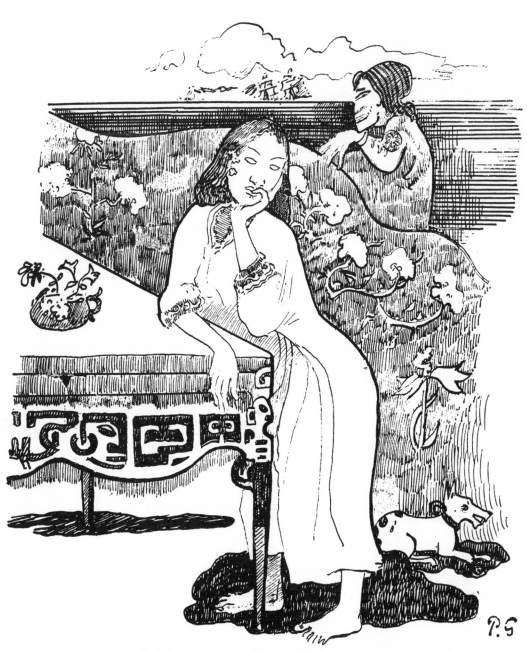

OF WHAT ARE YOU THINKING? I DO NOT KNOW

GAUGUIN'S
INTIMATE JOURNALS

Paul Gauguin

Translated by Van Wyck Brooks
Preface by Emil Gauguin

DOVER PUBLICATIONS, INC.
Mineola, New York

In order to preserve the complete text of *Gauguin's Intimate Journals*, the publisher regrets any prejudicial references or biased remarks that the present edition may contain.

Published in Canada by General Publishing Company, Ltd., 30 Lesmill Road, Don Mills, Toronto, Ontario.

Published in the United Kingdom by Constable and Company, Ltd., 3 The Lanchesters, 162–164 Fulham Palace Road, London W6 9ER.

Bibliographical Note

This Dover edition, first published in 1997, is an unabridged and slightly altered republication of the work originally published by Boni and Liveright, Inc., New York, in 1921, in an edition limited to 990 numbered copies. The original edition was privately printed for subscribers only under the title *Paul Gauguin's Intimate Journals*. Several full-page illustrations have been repositioned in the present edition.

Library of Congress Cataloging-in-Publication Data

Gauguin, Paul, 1848–1903.
    [Avant et après. English]
    Gauguin's intimate journals / Paul Gauguin ; translated by Van Wyck Brooks ; preface by Emil Gauguin.
        p.   cm.
    Previously published under title: Paul Gauguin's intimate journals.
    "An unabridged and slightly altered republication of the work originally published by Boni and Liveright, New York, 1921"—T.p. verso.
    ISBN 0-486-29441-2 (pbk.)
    1. Gauguin, Paul, 1848–1903—Diaries.   2. Painters—France—Diaries. I. Gauguin, Paul, 1848–1903. Paul Gauguin's intimate journals. II. Title.
ND553.G27A2   1996
759.4—dc20   96-38839
                                           CIP

Manufactured in the United States of America
Dover Publications, Inc., 31 East 2nd Street, Mineola, N.Y. 11501

TO MONSIEUR FONTAINAS

ALL THIS—ALL THAT

MOVED BY AN UNCONSCIOUS SENTIMENT BORN OF SOLITUDE AND
SAVAGERY—IDLE TALES OF A NAUGHTY CHILD WHO SOMETIMES
REFLECTS AND WHO IS ALWAYS A LOVER OF THE BEAUTIFUL—THE
BEAUTY THAT IS PERSONAL—THE ONLY BEAUTY THAT IS HUMAN.

PAUL GAUGUIN

PREFACE

A fantastic Gauguin legend, distorted in many retellings, has come into being. A legend far better known than his strikingly individual pictures are known, and, in this country, at least, discussed by thousands who are quite oblivious of my father's accredited rank as one of the greatest masters of painting.

Everywhere this story has captured the popular fancy. Once upon a time there was a middle-aged, somewhat commonplace and moderately successful stock broker. He had a wife and three children to whom he was extremely devoted. Neither his family nor his friends had cause to suspect that he entertained any other ambition than to finish his days as a prosperous business man and a good paterfamilias. Then one night he shed all his domestic virtues in his sleep. He awoke an inhuman monster. Gone was his love of family. Gone were his bourgeois ambitions and respectability. A burning fever to paint possessed him. So he fled to Paris, with never a thought or a care for his dependent family, and devoted himself to his newly adopted art in sublime defiance of academic tradition. And at last, finding civilization too irksome to be borne, he retired to Tahiti, where he lived and loved and painted and died like a savage.

It is a good story. It is a pity to contradict it, so many credulous souls have been entertained by it. But, alas, it is not true. My father's decision to become a painter was no such Jekyll-and-Hyde transformation. I have a drawing he made of my mother as early as 1873, the year of their marriage. Indeed, all his life he had dabbled with paints, much to my mother's annoyance, when on occasions he would use her best linen table-cloth for canvas or her finest petticoat for paint-rags. It was 1882 when he definitely renounced commerce for art. His determination was reached after due consultation with my mother. She agreed to let him go, not because she had faith in his genius, but because she respected his passion for art. It was brave of her. It meant that she was to assume the burden of maintaining and educating the children. "Sale bourgeoise," my father called her; but all his life he respected her profoundly.

During his wanderings he never quite lost touch with us. At irregular intervals he would write to us, demanding our news and sending us affectionate greetings. Once from Tahiti he even sent us a bundle of those curiously individual paintings of his, which were examined with indifference if not with scorn and thrust into an attic room. But he was rather annoyed when my mother, considering these canvases as a contribution to the support of her children, tried—in vain, alas—to sell them. Years later, I believe, a few were sold, at ridiculously low prices.

My last memory of him is singularly vivid. He had come up to Copenhagen to bid us adieu before his last trip to Tahiti. Never had he seemed more tranquil and tender. Doubtless he was very happy at the prospect of returning to his tropical paradise. As a parting gift he gave me a portrait Eugene Carrière had painted of him that year. An excellent likeness, I have it still.

He was in the Marquesas when these journals were completed. He sent them to M. André Fontainas with a request to have them published after his death, or, if that were not possible, to keep them as a token of Paul Gauguin's esteem. M. Fontainas did not find a publisher, and so the journals, *per fas et nefas*, came into the possession of my mother and younger brother. After my mother's death I am presenting them in turn to the English reading public. Sales bourgeois—perhaps.

These journals, as far as I have been able to discover, are my father's longest single essay in the art of literature. "Noa Noa" was revised by M. Charles Morice from my father's manuscript and, I am afraid, hardly preserves the spirit of my father's work. Compare its style with the style of these journals or with the occasional essays on art subjects my father contributed to the French magazines, and the difference will be plain. For to me, at least, these journals are an illuminating self-portrait of a unique personality. They transfigure and make vivid my recollections of my father, recollections all too dim and few. They bring sharply into focus for me his goodness, his humor, his insurgent spirit, his clarity of vision, his inordinate hatred of hypocricy and sham.

What others will make of them I do not know, and do not greatly care. All his life my father shocked smugly respectable people, shocked them deliberately and for the same impish reason that impelled him to hang on his wall that obscene picture he tells about in these journals. What is more fitting than that he should continue to shock them after his death?

The other sort of people will not misunderstand. They will not fail to perceive that these journals are the spontaneous expression of the same free, fearless, sensitive spirit that speaks in the canvases of Paul Gauguin.

EMIL GAUGUIN.

Philadelphia, May, 1921.

PAUL GAUGUIN'S
INTIMATE JOURNALS

This is not a book. A book, even a bad book, is a serious affair. A phrase that might be excellent in the fourth chapter would be all wrong in the second, and it is not everybody who knows the trick.

A novel—where does it begin, where does it end? The intelligent Camille Mauclair gives us this as its definitive form; the question is settled till a new Mauclair comes and announces to us a new form.

"True to life!" Isn't reality sufficient for us to dispense with writing about it? And besides, one changes. There was a time when I hated Georges Sand. Now Georges Ohnet makes her seem almost supportable to me. In the books of Emile Zola the washerwomen and the concierges speak a French that fills me with anything but enthusiasm. When they stop talking, Zola, without realizing it, continues in the same tone and in the same French.

I have no desire to speak ill of him. I am not a writer. I should like to write as I paint my pictures,—that is to say, following my fancy, following the moon, and finding the title long afterwards.

Memoirs! That means history, dates. Everything in them is interesting except the author. And one has to say who one is and where one comes from. To confess oneself in the manner of Jean Jacques Rousseau is a serious matter. If I tell you that, on my mother's side, I descend from a Borgia of Aragon, Viceroy of Peru, you will say it is not true and that I am giving myself airs. But if I tell you that this family is a family of scavengers, you will despise me.

If I tell you that, on my father's side, they are all called Gauguin, you will say that this is absolutely childish; if I explain myself on the subject, with the idea of convincing you that I am not a bastard, you will smile sceptically.

The best thing would be to hold my tongue, but it is a strain to hold one's tongue when one is full of a desire to talk. Some people have an end in life, others have none. For a long time I had virtue dinned into me; I know all about that but I do not like it. Life is hardly more than the fraction of a second. Such a little time to prepare oneself for eternity!!!

I should like to be a pig: man alone can be ridiculous.

Once upon a time the wild animals, the big ones, used to roar; today they are stuffed. Yesterday I belonged to the nineteenth century; today I belong to the twentieth and I assure you that you and I are not going to see the twenty-first. Life being what it is, one dreams of revenge—and has to content oneself with dreaming. Yet I am not one of those who speak ill of life. You suffer, but you also enjoy, and however brief that enjoyment has been, it is the thing you remember. I like the philosophers, except when they bore me or when they are pedantic. I like women, too; when they are fat and vicious; their intelligence annoys me; it's too spiritual for me. I have always wanted a mistress who was fat and I have never found one. To make a fool of me, they are always pregnant.

This does not mean that I am not susceptible to beauty, but simply that my senses will have none of it. As you perceive, I do not know love. To say "I love you" would break all my teeth. So much to show you that I am anything but a poet. A poet without love!! Women, who are shrewd, divine this, and for this reason I repel them.

I have no complaint to make. Like Jesus I say, The flesh is the flesh, the spirit is the spirit. Thanks to this, a small sum of money satisfies my flesh and my spirit is left in peace.

Here I am, then, offered to the public like an animal, stripped of all sentiment, incapable of selling his soul for any Gretchen. I have not been a Werther, and I shall not be a Faust. Who knows? The syphilitic and the alcoholic will perhaps be the men of the future. It looks to me as if morality, like the sciences and all the rest, were on its way toward a quite new morality which will perhaps be the opposite of that of today. Marriage, the family, and ever so many good things which they din into my ears, seem to be dashing off at full speed in an automobile.

Do you expect me to agree with you?

Whom one gets into bed with is no light matter.

In marriage, the greater cuckold of the two is the lover, whom a play at the Palais Royal calls "the luckiest of the three."

I had bought some photographs at Port Said. The sin committed—*ab ores*. They were set up quite frankly in an alcove in my quarters. Men, women and children laughed at them, nearly everyone, in fact; but it was a matter of a moment, and no one thought any more of it. Only the people who called themselves respectable stopped coming to my house, and they alone thought about it the whole year through. The bishop, at confession, made all sorts of enquiries; some of the nuns, even, turned paler and paler and grew hollow-eyed over it.

Think this over and nail up some indecency in plain sight over your door; from that time forward you will be rid of all respectable people, the most insupportable folk God has created.

I have known, everyone knows, everyone will continue to know, that two and two make four. It is a long way from convention, from mere intuition, to real understanding. I agree, and like everyone else I say, "Two and two make four." . . . But this irritates me; it quite upsets my way of thinking. Thus, for example, you who insist that two and two make four, as if it were a certainty that could not possibly be otherwise,—why do you also maintain that God is the creator of everything? If only for an instant, could not God have arranged things differently?

A strange sort of Almighty!

All this apropos of pedants. We know and we do not know.

The Holy Shroud of Jesus revolts M. Berthelot. Of course the learned chemist Berthelot may be right; but of course the Pope. . . . Come, my charming Berthelot, what would you do if you were Pope, a man whose feet are kissed? Thousands of imbeciles demand the benediction of all these Lourdes. Someone has to be the Pope and a Pope must bless and satisfy all his faithful. Not every one is a chemist. I, myself, know nothing about such matters, and perhaps if I ever have hemorrhoids I shall set about plotting how to get a fragment of this Holy Shroud to poke it into myself, convinced that it will cure me.

This is not a book.

Besides, even if he has no serious readers, the author of a book must be serious.

I have here before me some cocoanut and banana trees; they are all green. I will tell you, to please Signac, that little spots of red (the complementary colour) are scattered through the green. In spite of that—and this will displease Signac—I can swear that all through this green one observes great patches of blue. Don't mistake this; it is not the blue sky but only the mountain in the distance. What can I say to all these cocoanut trees? And yet I must chatter; so I write instead of talking.

Look! There is little Vaitauni on her way to the river. . . . She has the roundest and most charming breasts you can imagine. I see this golden, almost naked body make its way toward the fresh water. Take care, dear child, the hairy gendarme, guardian of the public morals, who is a faun in secret, is watching you. When he is satisfied with staring he will charge you with a misdemeanour in revenge for having troubled his senses and so outraged public morals. Public morals! What words!

Oh! good people of the metropolis, you have no idea what a gendarme is in the colonies! Come here and look for yourselves; you will see indecencies of a sort you could not have imagined.

But having seen little Vaitauni I feel my senses beginning to boil. I set off for some amusement in the river. We have both of us laughed, without bothering about fig-leaves and   .   .   .

This is not a book.

Let me tell you something that happened long ago.

General Boulanger, you may remember, was once hiding in Jersey. Just at this time—it was winter—I was working in Pouldu on the lonely coast at the end of Finistère, far, very far from any farmhouses.

A gendarme turned up with orders to watch the coast to prevent the supposed landing of General Boulanger in the disguise of a fisherman.

I was shrewdly questioned and so turned inside out that, quite intimidated, I exclaimed: "Do you by any chance take me for General Boulanger?"

He—"We have seen stranger things than that."

I—"Have you his description?"

He—"His description? It strikes me that you're a bit impudent. I'd better just take you along."

I was obliged to go to Quimperlé to explain myself. The police-sergeant proved to me immediately that, since I was not General Boulanger, I had no right to pass myself off for the general and make fun of a gendarme in the exercise of his duties.

What! I pass myself off for the general?

"You will have to admit that you did," said the sergeant, "since the gendarme took you for Boulanger."

As for me, I was not so much stupefied as filled with admiration for such a magnificent intelligence. It was like saying that one is more easily taken in by imbeciles. I don't want to be told that I am repeating La Fontaine's fable about the bear. What I say has quite another meaning. Having done my military service, I have observed that non-commissioned officers, and even some officers, grow angry when you speak to them in French, thinking, no doubt, that it is a language meant for making fun of people and humiliating them.

Which proves that, in order to live in the world, one must be especially on one's guard against small folk. One often has need of someone humbler than oneself. No, not that! I should say one often has reason to fear someone humbler than oneself. In the antechamber, the flunkey stands in front of the minister.

Having been recommended by someone of importance, a young man asked a minister for a position, and found himself promptly bowed out. But his shoemaker was the minister's shoemaker! . . . Nothing was refused him!

With a woman who feels pleasure I feel twice as much pleasure.
The Censor—Pornography!
The Author—Hypocritography!

Question: Do you know Greek?
Reply: Why should I? I have only to read Pierre Louÿs. But if Pierre Louÿs writes excellent French it is just because he knows Greek so well.

As to morals, they well deserve what has been written by the Jesuits:

Digitus tertius, digitus diaboli.

What the devil, are we cocks or capons? Must we come to the artificial laying of eggs? *Spiritus sanctus!*

Marriage is beginning to make its appearance in this country: an attempt to regularize things. Imported Christians have set their hearts upon this singular business.

The gendarme exercises the functions of the mayor. Two couples, converted to the idea of matrimony, and dressed in brand new clothes, listen to the reading of the matrimonial laws; with the "yes" once uttered they are married. As they go out, one of the two males says to the other, "Suppose we exchange?" And very gaily each goes off with a new wife to the church, where the bells fill the air with merriment.

The bishop, with the eloquence that characterizes missionaries, thunders against adulterers and then blesses the new union which in this holy place is already the beginning of an adultery.

Or again, as they are going out of the church, the groom says to the maid of honour, "How pretty you are!" And the bride says to the best man, "How handsome you are!" Very soon one couple moves off to the right and another to the left, deep into the underbrush where, in the shelter of the banana trees and before the Almighty, two marriages take place instead of one. Monseigneur is satisfied and says, "We are beginning to civilize them. . . ."

On a little island of which I have forgotten the name and the latitude, a bishop exercises his profession of Christian moralization. He is a regular goat, they say. In spite of the austerity of his heart and his senses, he loves a school-girl,—paternally, purely. Unfortunately, the devil sometimes meddles with things that do not concern him, and one fine day our bishop, walking in the wood, catches sight of this beloved child quite naked in the river, washing her chemise.

> Petite Thérèse, on the river bank,
> Washed her chemise in the running water.
> It was spotted by an accident
> Which happens to little girls twelve times a year.

"*Tiens*," he said, "but she is just at the point. . . ."

I can well believe she was at the point! Just ask the fifteen vigorous young men who that very evening enjoyed her embraces. At the sixteenth, she hung back.

The adorable child was married to the beadle who lived in the enclosure. Neat and brisk, she swept out the bishop's bedroom and saw to the incense.

At divine service the husband held the candle.

How unkind the world is! Evil tongues began to wag and I, for one, was profoundly convinced of what they said when a pious Catholic woman remarked to me one day:

"*Vois-tu*" (and at the same time without a wink she emptied a glass of rum); "*vois-tu, mon petit*, it's all nonsense about the bishop's sleeping with Thérèse; he merely confesses her to try to appease his passion."

Thérèse was the queen bean. Don't try to understand. I'll explain it to you.

On the Epiphany, Monseigneur had had a superb cake made by the Chinaman. Thérèse's slice had contained a bean, so that she was made the queen, Monseigneur being the king. From that day on Thérèse continued to be the queen and the beadle the husband of the queen.

But alas! the famous bean grew old, and our goat, who was a sly one, found a new bean a few miles further off.

Imagine a Chinese bean, as plump as possible. Anyone would have eaten it.

You, painter in search of a gracious subject, take your brushes and immortalize this picture: our goat, with his episcopal trappings, well planted in the saddle, and his bean, whose curves both before and behind would be enough to bring to life a pope's choir-boy. And besides, one whose chemise . . . you understand . . . it is useless to repeat. Four times he got down off his horse. And Picpus' money-box was lightened by ten piastres.

There's gossip for you . . . but . . .

This is not a book.

For a long time I have wanted to write about Van Gogh, and I shall certainly do so some fine day when I am in the mood. I am going to tell you now a few rather timely things about him, or rather about us, in order to correct an error which has been going round in certain circles.

It so happens that several men who have been a good deal in my company and in the habit of discussing things with me have gone mad.

This was true of the two Van Gogh brothers, and certain malicious persons and others have childishly attributed their madness to me. Undoubtedly some men have more or less influence over their friends, but there is a great difference between that and causing madness. A long time after the catastrophe, Vincent wrote me, from the private asylum where he was being cared for. He said, "How fortunate you are to be in Paris. That is where one finds the best doctors, and you certainly ought to consult a specialist to cure your madness. Aren't we all mad?" The advice was good and that was why I didn't follow it,—from a spirit of contradiction, I dare say.

Readers of the *Mercure* may have noticed in a letter of Vincent's, published a few years ago, the insistence with which he tried to get me to come to Arles to found an atelier after an idea of his own, of which I was to be the director.

At that time I was working at Pont-Aven, in Brittany, and either because the studies I had begun attached me to this spot, or because a vague instinct forewarned me of something abnormal, I resisted a long time, till the day came when, finally overborne by Vincent's sincere, friendly enthusiasm, I set out on my journey.

I arrived at Arles toward the end of the night and waited for dawn in a little all-night café. The proprietor looked at me and exclaimed, "You are the pal, I recognize you!"

A portrait of myself which I had sent to Vincent explains the proprietor's exclamation. In showing him my portrait Vincent had told him that it was a pal of his who was coming soon.

Neither too early nor too late I went to rouse Vincent out. The day was devoted to my getting settled, to a great deal of talking and to walking about so that I might admire the beauty of Arles and the Arlesian women, about whom, by the way, I could not get up much enthusiasm.

The next day we were at work, he continuing what he had begun, and I starting something new. I must tell you that I have never had the mental facility that others find, without any trouble, at the tips of their brushes. These fellows get off the train, pick up their palette and turn you off a sunlight effect at once. When it is dry it goes to the Luxembourg and is signed Carolus-Duran.

I don't admire the painting but I admire the man. He so confident, so calm. I so uncertain, so uneasy.

Wherever I go I need a certain period of incubation, so that I may learn every time the essence of the plants and trees, of all nature, in short, which never wishes to be understood or to yield herself.

So it was several weeks before I was able to catch distinctly the sharp flavour of Arles and its surroundings. But that did not hinder our working hard, especially Vincent. Between two such beings as he and I, the one a perfect volcano, the other boiling too, inwardly, a sort of struggle was preparing. In the first place, everywhere and in everything I found a disorder that shocked me. His colour-box could hardly contain all those tubes, crowded together and never closed. In spite of all this disorder, this mess, something shone out of his canvasses and out of his talk, too. Daudet, Goncourt, the Bible fired his Dutch brain. At Arles, the quays, the bridges, the ships, the whole Midi took the place of Holland to him. He even forgot how to write Dutch and, as may be seen in his published letters to his brother, never wrote anything but French, admirable French, with no end of *whereases* and *inasmuches*.

In spite of all my efforts to disentangle from this disordered brain a reasoned logic in his critical opinions, I could not explain to myself the utter contradiction between his painting and his opinions. Thus, for example, he had an unlimited admiration for Meissonier and a profound

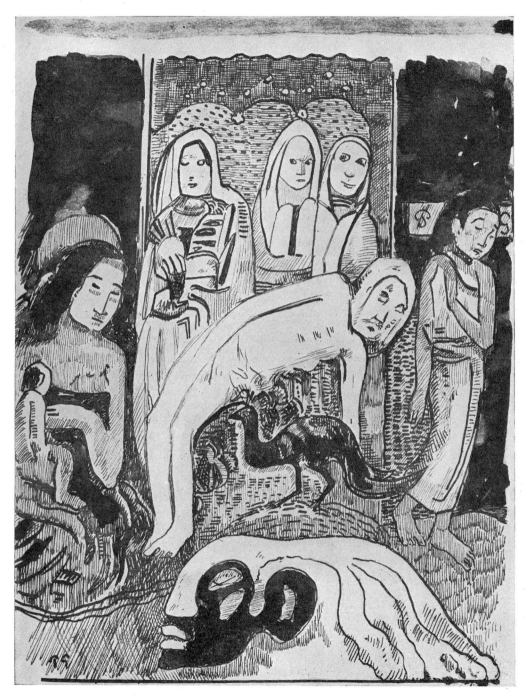

THE HOLY IMAGES

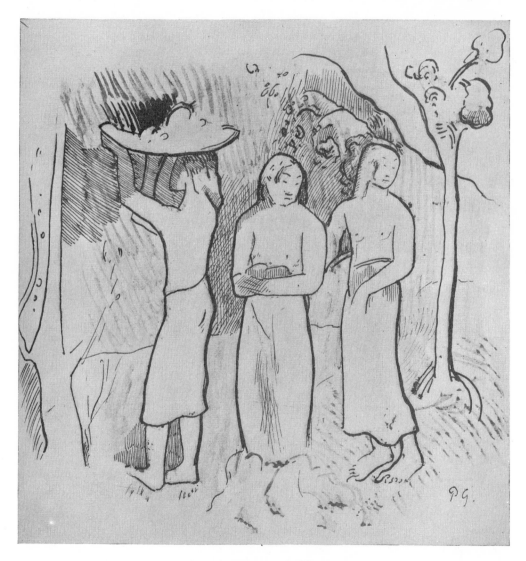

ON THE WAY TO THE FEAST

hatred for Ingres. Degas was his despair and Cézanne nothing but a faker. When he thought of Monticelli he wept.

One thing that angered him was to have to admit that I had plenty of intelligence, although my forehead was too small, a sign of imbecility. Along with all this, he possessed the greatest tenderness, or rather the altruism of the Gospel.

From the very first month I saw that our common finances were taking on the same appearance of disorder. What was I to do? The situation was delicate, as the cash-box was only very modestly filled (by his brother, a clerk at Goupil's, and on my side through an exchange of pictures). I was obliged to speak, at the risk of wounding that very great susceptibility of his. It was thus with many precautions and much gentle coaxing, of a sort very foreign to my nature, that I approached the question. I must confess that I succeeded far more easily than I should have supposed.

We kept a box,—so much for hygienic excursions at night, so much for tobacco, so much for incidental expenses, including rent. On top of it lay a scrap of paper and a pencil for us to write down virtuously what each took from this chest. In another box was the rest of the money, divided into four parts, to pay for our food each week. We gave up our little restaurant, and I did the cooking, on a gas-stove, while Vincent laid in the provisions, not going very far from the house. Once, however, Vincent wanted to make a soup. How he mixed it I don't know; as he mixed his colours in his pictures, I dare say. At any rate, we couldn't eat it. And my Vincent burst out laughing and exclaimed: *"Tarascon! la casquette au père Daudet!"* On the wall he wrote in chalk:

Je suis Saint Esprit.
Je suis sain d'esprit.

How long did we remain together? I couldn't say, I have entirely forgotten. In spite of the swiftness with which the catastrophe approached, in spite of the fever of work that had seized me, the time seemed to me a century.

Though the public had no suspicion of it, two men were performing there a colossal work that was useful to them both. Perhaps to others? There are some things that bear fruit.

Vincent, at the time when I arrived in Arles, was in the full current of the Neo-impressionist school, and was floundering about a good deal and suffering as a result of it; not because this school, like all schools, was bad, but because it did not correspond to his nature, which was so far from patient and so independent.

9

With all these yellows on violets, all this work in complementary colours,. a disordered work on his part, he accomplished nothing but the mildest of incomplete and monotonous harmonies. The sound of the trumpet was missing in them.

I undertook the task of enlightening him,—an easy matter, for I found a rich and fertile soil. Like all original natures that are marked with the stamp of personality, Vincent had no fear of the other man and was not stubborn.

From that day my Van Gogh made astonishing progress; he seemed to divine all that he had in him, and the result was that whole series of sun-effects over sun-effects in full sunlight.

Have you seen the portrait of the poet?

The face and hair are chrome yellow (1).

The clothes are chrome yellow (2).

The necktie is chrome yellow (3) with an emerald scarfpin, on a background of chrome yellow (4).

That is what an Italian painter said to me, and he added: "*Marde! marde!* Everything is yellow! I don't know what painting is any longer!"

It would be idle to enter here into questions of technique. This is only to let you know that Van Gogh, without losing an ounce of his originality, learned a fruitful lesson from me. And every day he thanked me for it. That is what he means when he writes to M. Aurier that he owes much to Paul Gauguin.

When I arrived at Arles, Vincent was trying to find himself, while I, who was a good deal older, was a mature man. But I owe something to Vincent, and that is, in the consciousness of having been useful to him, the confirmation of my own original ideas about painting. And also, at difficult moments, the remembrance that one finds others unhappier than oneself.

When I read this remark, "Gauguin's drawing somewhat recalls that of Van Gogh," I smile.

During the latter days of my stay, Vincent would become excessively rough and noisy, and then silent. On several nights I surprised him in the act of getting up and coming over to my bed. To what can I attribute my awakening just at that moment?

At all events, it was enough for me to say to him, quite sternly, "What's the matter with you, Vincent?" for him to go back to bed without a word and fall into a heavy sleep.

The idea occurred to me to do his portrait while he was painting the still-life he loved so much—some ploughs. When the portrait was finished, he said to me, "It is certainly I, but it's I gone mad."

That very evening we went to the café. He took a light absinthe. Suddenly he flung the glass and its contents at my head. I avoided the blow and, taking him bodily in my arms, went out of the café, across the Place Victor Hugo. Not many minutes later Vincent found himself in his bed where, in a few seconds, he was asleep, not to awaken again till morning.

When he awoke, he said to me very calmly, "My dear Gauguin, I have a vague memory that I offended you last evening."

Answer: "I forgive you gladly and with all my heart, but yesterday's scene might occur again and if I were struck I might lose control of myself and give you a choking. So permit me to write to your brother and tell him that I am coming back."

My God, what a day!

When evening had come and I had bolted my dinner, I felt I must go out alone and take the air along some paths that were bordered by flowering laurel. I had almost crossed the Place Victor Hugo when I heard behind me a well-known step, short, quick, irregular. I turned about on the instant as Vincent rushed toward me, an open razor in his hand. My look at that moment must have had great power in it, for he stopped and, lowering his head, set off running towards home.

Was I negligent on this occasion? Should I have disarmed him and tried to calm him? I have often questioned my conscience about this, but I have never found anything to reproach myself with. Let him who will fling the stone at me.

With one bound I was in a good Arlesian hotel, where, after I had enquired the time, I engaged a room and went to bed.

I was so agitated that I could not get to sleep till about three in the morning, and I awoke rather late, at about half-past seven.

Reaching the square, I saw a great crowd collected. Near our house there were some gendarmes and a little gentleman in a melon-shaped hat who was the superintendent of police.

This is what had happened.

Van Gogh had gone back to the house and had immediately cut off his ear close to the head. He must have taken some time to stop the flow of blood, for the day after there were a lot of wet towels lying about on the flag-stones in the two lower rooms. The blood had stained the two rooms and the little stairway that led up to our bedroom.

When he was in a condition to go out, with his head enveloped in a Basque *beret* which he had pulled far down, he went straight to a certain house where for want of a fellow-countrywoman one can pick up an acquaintance, and gave the manager his ear, carefully washed and placed in an envelope. "Here is a souvenir of me," he said. Then he ran off home, where he went to bed and to sleep. He took pains, however, to close the blinds and set a lighted lamp on a table near the window.

Ten minutes later the whole street assigned to the *filles de joie* was in commotion and they were chattering over what had happened.

I had no faintest suspicion of all this when I presented myself at the door of our house and the gentleman in the melon-shaped hat said to me abruptly and in a tone that was more than severe, "What have you done to your comrade, Monsieur?"

"I don't know. . . ."

"Oh, yes . . . you know very well . . . he is dead."

I could never wish anyone such a moment, and it took me a long time to get my wits together and control the beating of my heart.

Anger, indignation, grief, as well as shame at all these glances that were tearing my person to pieces, suffocated me, and I answered, stammeringly: "All right, Monsieur, let us go upstairs. We can explain ourselves there."

In the bed lay Vincent, rolled up in the sheets, humped up like a gun-cock; he seemed lifeless. Gently, very gently, I touched the body, the heat of which showed that it was still alive. For me it was as if I had suddenly got back all my energy, all my spirit.

Then in a low voice I said to the police superintendent: "Be kind enough, Monsieur, to awaken this man with great care, and if he asks for me tell him I have left for Paris; the sight of me might prove fatal to him."

I must own that from this moment the police superintendent was as reasonable as possible and intelligently sent for a doctor and a cab.

Once awake, Vincent asked for his comrade, his pipe and his tobacco; he even thought of asking for the box that was downstairs and contained our money,—a suspicion, I dare say! But I had already been through too much suffering to be troubled by that.

Vincent was taken to a hospital where, as soon as he had arrived, his brain began to rave again.

All the rest everyone knows who has any interest in knowing it, and it would be useless to talk about it were it not for that great suffering of a man who, confined in a madhouse, at monthly intervals recovered his reason enough to understand his condition and furiously paint the admirable pictures we know.

The last letter I had from him was dated from Anvers, near Pontoise. He told me that he had hoped to recover enough to come and join me in Brittany, but that now he was obliged to recognize the impossibility of a cure:

"Dear Master" (the only time he ever used this word), "after having known you and caused you pain, it is better to die in a good state of mind than in a degraded one."

He sent a revolver shot into his stomach, and it was only a few hours later that he died, lying in his bed and smoking his pipe, having complete possession of his mind, full of the love of his art and without hatred for others.

In *Les Monstres* Jean Dolent writes, "When Gauguin says 'Vincent' his voice is gentle." Without knowing it but having guessed it, Jean Dolent is right.

You know why. . . . .

Scattered notes, without sequence, like dreams, like a life all made up of fragments; and because others have shared in it, the love of beautiful things seen in the houses of others. Things that are sometimes childish when they are written, some of them the fruits of one's leisure, some the classifications of beloved though perhaps foolish ideas,—in defiance of a bad memory, and some rays that pierce to the vital centre of my art. If a work of art were a work of chance, all these notes would be useless.

I believe that the thought which has guided my work, a part of my work, is mysteriously linked with a thousand other thoughts, some my own, some those of others. There are days of idle imagination from which I recall long studies, often sterile, more often troubling: a black cloud has just darkened the horizon; confusion overtakes my soul and I am unable to do anything. If in other hours of bright sunshine and a clear mind I attach myself to such and such a fact, or vision, or bit of reading, I feel I must make some brief record of it, perpetuate the memory of it.

Sometimes I have gone far back, farther back than the horses of the Parthenon . . . as far back as the Dada of my babyhood, the good rocking-horse.

I have lingered among the nymphs of Corot, dancing in the sacred wood of Ville-d'Avray.

This is not a book.

I have a cock with purple wings, a golden neck and a black tail. *Mon Dieu*, how fine he is! And he amuses me.

I have a silver-grey hen, with ruffled plumage; she scratches, she pecks, she destroys my flowers. It makes no difference. She is droll without being prudish. The cock makes a sign to her with his wings and feet and she immediately offers her rump. Slowly, vigorously too, he climbs on top of her.

Oh! it's quickly over! Is fortune favourable? I don't know.

The children laugh, I laugh. *Mon Dieu*, what idiocy! I am so poor I have nothing to put in my pot! If I ate the cock? And I am hungry. He would be too tough. The hen, then? But in that case I could no longer amuse myself watching my cock with the purple wings, the golden neck and the black tail climb on top of my hen; the children would not laugh any longer. I am still hungry.

The deluge! Once the angry sea rose to the highest peaks. And now the sea, appeased, licks the rocks.

In other words, *vois-tu, ma fille*, yesterday you climbed up, today you climb down. You go down thinking you are going up.

I owe a debt to society.
How much?
How much does society owe me?
A great deal too much.
Will it ever pay?
Never! (Liberty, Equality, Fraternity!)

On the veranda, a quiet siesta, everything peaceful. My eyes see the space before me without taking it in; and I have the sensation of something endless of which I am the beginning.

Moorea on the horizon; the sun is approaching it. I follow its mournful march; without comprehending it I have the sensation of a movement that is going to go on forever: a universal life that will never be extinguished.

And lo, the night. Everything is quiet. My eyes close, to see without grasping it the dream in infinite space that flees before me. And I have the sweet sensation of the mournful procession of my hopes.

We are dining. A long table. On either side are lines of plates and glasses. Set out in this way these plates, these glasses in perspective make the table seem long, very long. But this is a banquet.

Stéphane Mallarmé presides; opposite is Jean Moréas, the symbolist. The guests are symbolists. Perhaps they are lacqueys, too. Down there, far away, at the end is Clovis Lugnes (Marseilles). Far off also, at the other end, Barrès (Paris).

We are dining; there are toasts. The president begins; Moréas replies. Clovis Lugnes, ruddy, long-haired, exuberant, makes a long speech, naturally in verse.

Barrès, tall and slender, clean-shaven, quotes Baudelaire in a dry fashion, in prose. We listen. The marble is cold.

My neighbour, who is very young but stout (superb diamond buttons glitter on his many-pleated shirt), asks me in a low voice, "Is Monsieur Baudelaire with us tonight?"

I scratch my knee and answer, "Yes, he is here, down there among the poets. Barrès is talking with him."

He: "Oh! I should so much like to be introduced to him!"

Somewhere some saint says to one of his penitents: "Be on your guard against the pride of humility."

Letter from Strindberg:

You have set your heart on having the preface to your catalogue written by me, in memory of the winter of 1894–95 when we lived here behind the Institute, not far from the Pantheon and quite close to the cemetery of Montparnasse.

I should gladly have given you this souvenir to take away with you to that island in Oceania, where you are going to seek for space and a scenery in harmony with your powerful stature, but from the very beginning I feel myself in an equivocal position and I am replying at once to your request with an "I cannot," or, more brutally still, with an "I do not wish to."

At the same time I owe you an explanation of my refusal, which does not spring from a lack of friendly feeling, or from a lazy pen, although it would have been easy for me to place the blame on the trouble in my hands which, as a matter of fact, has not given the skin time to grow in the palms.

Here it is: I cannot understand your art and I cannot like it. I have no grasp of your art, which is now exclusively Tahitian. But I know that this confession will neither astonish nor wound you, for you always seem to me fortified especially by the hatred of others: your personality delights in the antipathy it arouses, anxious as it is to keep its own integrity. And perhaps this is a good thing, for the moment you were approved and admired and had supporters, they would classify you, put you in your place and give your art a name which, five years later, the younger generation would be using as a tag for designating a superannuated art, an art they would do everything to render still more out of date.

I myself have made many serious attempts to classify you, to introduce you like a link into the chain, so that I might understand the history of your development, but in vain.

I remember my first stay in Paris, in 1876. The city was a sad one, for the nation was mourning over the events that had occurred and was anxious about the future; something was fermenting.

In the circle of Swedish artists we had not yet heard the name of Zola, for *L'Assommoir* was still to be published. I was present at a performance at the Théâtre Français of *Rome Vaincue*, in which Mme. Sarah Bernhardt, the new star, was crowned as a second Rachel, and my young artists had dragged me over to Durand-Ruel's to see something quite new in painting. A young painter who was then unknown was my guide and we saw some marvelous canvasses, most of them signed Monet and Manet. But as I had other things to do in Paris than to look at pictures (as the secretary of the Library of Stockholm it was my task to hunt up an old Swedish missal in the library of Sainte-Geneviève), I looked at this new painting with calm indifference. But the next day I returned, I did not know just why, and I discovered that there was "something" in these bizarre manifestations. I saw the swarming of a crowd over a pier, but I did not see the crowd itself; I saw the rapid passage of a train across a Normandy landscape, the movement of wheels in the street, frightful portraits of excessively ugly persons who had not known how to pose calmly. Very much struck by these canvasses, I sent to a paper in my own country a letter in which I tried to explain the sensation I thought the Impressionists had tried to render, and my article had a certain success as a piece of incomprehensibility.

When, in 1883, I returned to Paris a second time, Manet was dead, but his spirit lived in a whole school that struggled for hegemony with Bastien-Lepage. During my third stay in Paris, in 1885, I saw the Manet exhibition. This movement had now forced itself to the front; it had produced its effect and it was now classified. At the triennial exposition, which occurred that very year, there was an utter anarchy—all styles, all colours, all subjects, historical, mythological and naturalistic. People no longer wished to hear of schools or tendencies. Liberty was now the rallying-cry. Taine had said that the beautiful was not the pretty, and Zola that art was a fragment of nature seen through a temperament.

Nevertheless, in the midst of the last spasms of naturalism, one name was pronounced by all with admiration, that of Puvis de Chavannes. He stood quite alone, like a contradiction, painting with a believing soul, even while he took a passing notice of the taste of his contemporaries for allusion. (We did not yet possess the term symbolism, a very unfortunate name for so old a thing as allegory.)

It was toward Puvis de Chavannes that my thoughts turned yesterday evening when, to the tropical sounds of the mandolin and the guitar, I saw on the walls of your studio that confused mass of pictures, flooded with sunshine, which pursued me last night in my dreams. I saw trees such as no botanist could ever discover, animals the existence of which had never been suspected by Cuvier, and men whom you alone could have created, a sea that might have flowed out of a volcano, a sky which no God could inhabit.

"Monsieur," I said in my dream, "you have created a new heaven and a new earth, but I do not enjoy myself in the midst of your creation. It is too sun-drenched for me, who enjoy the play of light and shade. And in your paradise there dwells an Eve who is not my ideal—for I, myself, really have an ideal of a woman or two!" This morning I went to the Luxembourg to have a look at Chavannes, who kept coming to my mind. I contemplated with profound sympathy the poor fisherman, so attentively occupied with watching for the catch that will bring him the faithful love of his wife, who is gathering flowers, and his idle child. That is beautiful! But now I am striking against the crown of thorns, Monsieur, which I hate, as you must know! I will have none of this pitiful God who accepts blows. My God is rather that Vitsliputski who in the sun devours the hearts of men.

No, Gauguin is not formed from the side of Chavannes, any more than from Manet's or Bastien-Lepage's!

What is he then? He is Gauguin, the savage, who hates a whimpering civilization, a sort of Titan who, jealous of the Creator, makes in his leisure hours his own little crea-

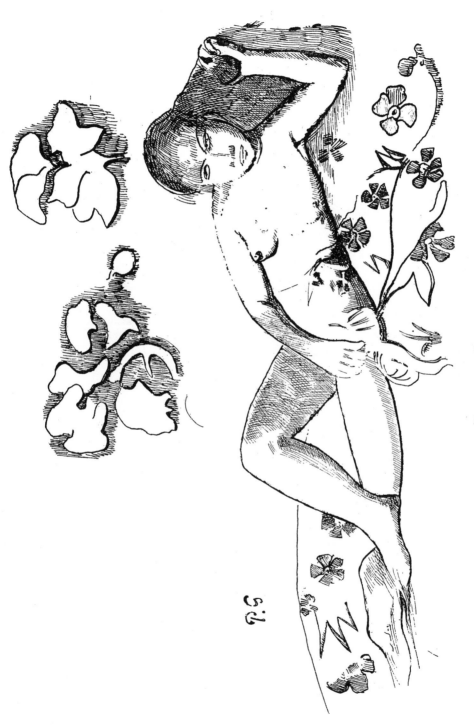

Decorative Figure

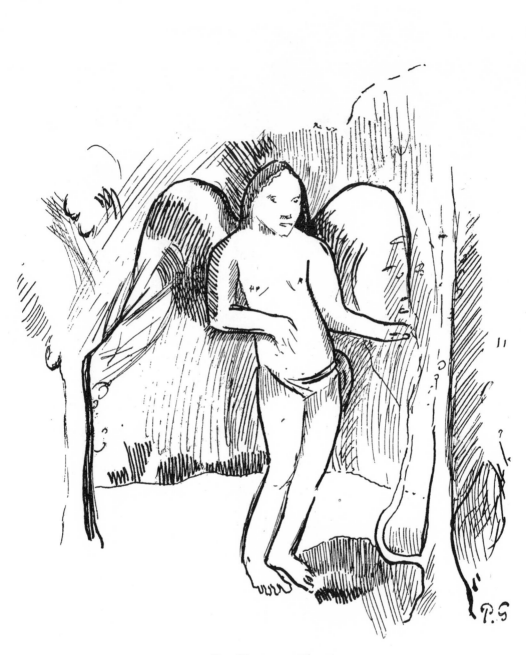

The Wings are Heavy

tion, the child who takes his toys to pieces so as to make others from them, who abjures and defies, preferring to see the heavens red rather than blue with the crowd.

Really, it seems to me that since I have warmed up as I write I am beginning to have a certain understanding of the art of Gauguin.

A modern author has been reproached for not depicting real beings, but for quite simply creating his personages himself. Quite simply!

Bon voyage, Master; but come back to us and come and see me. By then, perhaps, I shall have learned to understand your art better, which will enable me to write a real preface for a new catalogue in the Hotel Drouot. For I, too, am beginning to feel an immense need to become a savage and create a new world.

August Strindberg.

By Achille Delaroche:
Concerning the Painter Paul Gauguin, from an Aesthetic Point of View.

It would not be fitting for me to survey in its technical aspect the painting of Paul Gauguin. That is the affair of the painters, his rivals. But aside from the fact that an artist is often less impartially appreciated by his peers than by an outsider, it seems to me that there is a certain interest in having the workers in the neighbouring arts reach an understanding on the main lines of general aesthetics.

It is not therefore in any spirit of dilettantism that I shall erect, in this simple causerie, on fanciful foundations, to be sure, this vision of colour and design that has sprung up so ideally but also with so many significant signs of a method that is of interest to us all, dreamers and artists alike.

There is no longer any doubt, today, that the different arts, painting, poetry, music, after having followed separately their long and glorious courses, have been seized with a sudden malaise that has made them burst their dreary, time-honoured traditions, too narrow today, and are spreading out as if to mingle their waves in a single great current and overflow the surrounding territories.

Upon the ruins of venerable edifices and their synthesis, a whole aesthetic world is rising, a strange, paradoxical world, without defined rules, without classifications, with floating and inexact boundaries, but all the richer, intenser and more powerful because it is without limits and capable of stirring the human being to the very innermost and secret fibres of his spirit.

The strict guardians of the temple, overwhelmed by this cataclysm and powerless to make use of the little labels they love to paste on the back of every intellectual manifestation, are much distressed, but what is to be done about it? Does one measure the wave and define the tempest? Some, who reveal little enough aptitude for spirituality themselves, believe they can stem it by playing their poor, childish little tunes, as if the ridiculous had any place in art! Others mournfully invoke the Esprit Gaulois, the Latin race, Greek education, etc., which are beside the point, and imagine they have demonstrated by A plus B that this evolution is illegitimate and will finally prove to be an abortion. Nevertheless, irrefragable rebuffs have reached them from all sides: from the musical lyricism of Wagner and his school, from the poems of the Symbolist writers, from canvasses filled with wonder by recent painters.

Among these latter a high and quite individual place must be given to Paul Gauguin, not only because of his priority but because of the newness of his art. It was through the enchantments of a fairyland of light that we walked at the time of the recent exhibition to which he invited us, a light so dazzlingly intense that it seemed impossible, when we came out, to consider otherwise than as twilight effects, in contrast, the canvasses of our ordinary image-makers.

Gauguin is the painter of primitive natures; he loves them and possesses their simplicity, their suggestion of the hieratic, their somewhat awkward and angular naivety. His personages share the unstudied spontaneity of the virgin flora. It was only logical, therefore, that he should have exalted for our visual delight the riches of this tropical vegetation where a free life of Eden luxuriates under the happy stars: expressed here with an enchanting magic of colour, without any useless ornamentation or redundancy or Italianism.

It is sober, grandiose, imposing. And how the serenity of these natives overwhelms the vanity of our insipid elegancies, our childish agitations! All the mystery of the infinite moves behind the naive perversity of these eyes of theirs, opened to the freshness of things.

It makes little difference to me whether or not there is in these paintings any exact reproduction of the exotic reality. Gauguin makes use of this extraordinary setting in order to give his dream a local habitation, and what more favourable scene could there be than this, unpolluted as it still is by the lies of our civilization!

From these human figures, this blazing flora, the fantastic and the marvelous spring forth quite as well or better than they do from the chimeras and mythological attributes of others. It was the fashion, just then, to burst out laughing before the scandal of these really too monkey-like and far from animated anatomies, before these vertical landscapes which lack the spaciousness of a sufficient perspective. Could one deform nature in this way? And people gratuitously invoked the habitual eurythmy of Greek sculpture and Italian painting. But aside from the fact that it would be easy to recall Egyptian, Japanese, Gothic art, which took little account of these so-called indefeasible laws, the Dutch school, at the time when classicism was in full flower, certainly demonstrated that the ugly can also be the aesthetic. So it would be well to ignore the prejudices of our academies, with their correct lines, their stereotyped settings, their rhetoric of the torso, if one wishes to have a just appreciation of this strange art.

Although plastic art, according in this with the literary art and metaphysics, once held to the strict domain of formal and objective definition: the commemoration of the features of the hero or the bourgeois, the illustration of such and such a landscape, the rendering perceptible and distinct of natural or superior forces, this was and could not have been otherwise than through an ensemble of preconceived lines expressing this category of the ideal. Thus, we had the Discobolus, the Venus Genetrix, the Apollos with their harmonious gestures, Raphael's Madonnas, etc., which people our museums and put to shame the incoherent dissertations of the professors of aesthetics. But today, when a subtler life of thought has penetrated the different manifestations of the creative spirit, the anecdotic and special point of view yields place to the significant and the general. A gracious torso, a pure face, a picturesque landscape, appear to us as the magnificent and multiform flowerings of a single force, unknown and indefinable in itself, but the feeling of which asserts itself irresistibly in our consciousness. The artist will interest us less, therefore, by a vision tyrannically imposed and circumscribed, however harmonious it may be, than by a power of suggestion that is capable of aiding the flight of the imagination or of serving as the decorator of our own dreams, opening a new door on the infinite and the mystery of things.

Gauguin, better than anyone else thus far, seems to us to have understood this rôle of suggestive decoration. His procedure is notably characterized by a curtailing of particular features, by the synthesis of impressions. Each of his pictures is a general idea, though there is in it not enough observation of formal reality for the verisimilitude to strike us. And in no work of art does one find a better exteriorization of the constant concordance between the state of the soul and the landscape so luminously formulated by Baudelaire. If he represents jealousy for us it is by a blaze of pinks and violets in which all nature seems to participate, as if consciously and tacitly. If mysterious waters gush from lips thirsty for the unknown, it will be in an arena of strange colours, in the ripples on some diabolical or divine beverage, one does not know which. Here a fantastic orchard offers its insidious blossoms to the desire of an Eve, whose arms are extended timorously to pluck the flower of evil, while the quivering red wings of the chimera flutter about her forehead. Here it is the luxuriant forest of life and spring; wandering figures appear, far away, in a fortunate calm that knows no care; fabulous peacocks display their glittering feathers of sapphire and emerald; but the fateful axe of the woodcutter breaks in, striking the boughs, and behind him rises a faint filament of smoke, a warning of the transitory destiny of this fête. Here again, in a legendary landscape, rises the formidable, hieratic idol, and the tribute of the leaves streams in waves of colour over his brow; idyllic children sing on their pastoral flutes the infinite happiness of Eden, while at their feet, quiet, charmed, like evil genii watching, lie the heraldic red dogs. Further off, a stained-glass window full of richly-coloured flowers, human flowers and flowers of plants; with her divine child on her shoulder, an aureoled apparition of a woman, before whom two others clasp hands amid the blossoms, with the gestures of a seraph, exhaling mystic words as if from a miraculous chalice. Supernatural vegetation that prays, flesh that blossoms, on the indeterminate threshold of the conscious and the unconscious.

All these canvasses, and others still, offering similar suggestions, sufficiently show the intimate correlation in Gauguin of theme and form. But the masterly harmonization of colours in them is especially significant and completes the symbol. The tones contrast or melt into one another in gradations that sing like a symphony, in multiple and varied choruses and play a rôle that is truly orchestral.

Treated in this way colour, which as well as music is vibration, attains to what is most general and therefore most vague in nature: its inner force. It was quite logical, therefore, that in the present state of aesthetic feeling it should little by little take the place of design, which, in its suggestive value, falls to the second place.

Here appears definitely the goal toward which the different arts are tending, the place where they will meet perhaps: the future city of the spiritual life, to be built by them, of which poetry, as the state of the soul, would be the commanding gesture, music the atmosphere and painting the marvelous decoration. In fact, the scattered experiments that have been attempted hitherto have no significance except as the first rough draughts and as it were the divination of this era of ideal construction.

Humanity feels more or less obscurely that its present state of necessitous, quotidian reality is only transitory; and the hollow cracking of the old social forms is the significant indication of this impatience to establish finally, after the security of the instincts of nutrition, the disinterested play of a cerebrally sensitive life.

In its childhood, marvelling at the new mirage of things, it placed the enchanted palaces where dwelt the fairies among the inextricable bind-weeds of this exterior world. Then came the period of abstraction in which were formulated the scientific methods, rich in classifications, divisions and categories of every sort. Every object was taken apart, studied, weighed, dissected, defined. Proud of its dialectic, the human spirit came to consider it sophistically by itself and to believe it, as Kant did, the only reality. But the illusion was short-lived. Lofty thinkers flung far from them this vain instrument, the sterility of which is comparable to that of a machine that functions though it is empty. The mystics, on their side, not finding the satisfaction of sentiment in all this drought of syllogisms, had fallen back on ecstasy as a surer and more direct road to comprehension. But quite aside from the fact that this state is hardly accessible to the common run of people, and is a somewhat perilous intoxication, contemplative passivity leaves without an object all the active part of our natures.

The art that is held in consideration today, Orphic art, seems therefore about to take the place of the discursive modes of discredited thought and to lead us to the beautiful conquest, art that softens the wild beasts and moves in a harmonious cadence the shape-less creatures of the sea. Art, in fact, symbolizes nature, since it is creation; and this creation is tantamount to an idea, since to create is to comprehend. It thus includes in itself the connecting link between the conscious and the unconscious. So it is permitted us to hope that by a process analogous to the Intuition of Schelling, which was a glimpse of the truth, there will be formulated a sort of aesthetic agnosticism, magnifying the supreme Olympus of our dreams, Gods or Heroes.

Among all the others, painting is the art that will prepare the way by resolving the antinomy between the sensible and the intellectual worlds. And in the presence of a work such as that of Gauguin one begins to imagine those truly Enlightened Ones, not the maniacal idiots whom we know today, the collectors of silly knick-knacks, the purveyors of hysteria and Chinese fireworks, but beautifully intellectual spirits who, with a free fantasy, will weave the tapestry of their dreams. There the luminous frescoes of a Gauguin will represent the mural landscape, in which the symphonies of a Beethoven or a Schumann will sing their mysteries, while the sacred words of the poets will solemnly chant the spiritual legend of the human Odyssey.

A. Delaroche.

THE PINK SHRIMPS

Winter of '86

The snow is beginning to fall, it is winter. I will spare you the shroud, it is simply the snow. The poor are suffering. The landlords often do not understand that.

On this December day, in the rue Lepic of our good city of Paris, the pedestrians are in more than usual haste, having no desire to stroll. Among them is a fantastically dressed, shivering man who is hurrying to reach the outer boulevards. He is wrapped in a sheepskin coat with a cap that is undoubtedly of rabbit-fur and he has a bristling red beard. He looks like a drover.

Do not take a mere half-look; cold as it is, do not go on your way without carefully observing the white, graceful hand and those blue eyes that are so clear and childlike. It is some poor beggar, surely.

His name is Vincent Van Gogh.

Hurriedly he goes into a shop where they sell old ironwork, arrows of savages and cheap oil paintings.

Poor artist! You have put a fragment of your soul into this canvas which you have come to sell!

It is a small still-life, pink shrimps on a piece of pink paper.

"Can you give me a little money for this canvas to help me pay my rent?"

"*Mon Dieu*, my friend, my trade is getting difficult too. They ask me for cheap Millets! Then, you know," adds the shopkeeper, "your painting is not very gay. The Renaissance is the thing nowadays. Well, they say you have talent and I should like to do something for you. Come, here are a hundred sous."

And the round coin rings on the counter. Van Gogh takes it without a murmur, thanks the shopkeeper and goes out. He makes his way painfully back up the rue Lepic. When he has nearly reached his lodging a poor woman, just out of St. Lazare, smiles at the painter, hoping for his patronage. The beautiful white hand emerges from the overcoat. Van Gogh is a reader, he is thinking of the girl Elisa, and his five-franc piece becomes the unhappy woman's property. Quickly, as if ashamed of his charity, he makes off with an empty stomach.

A day will come, I see it as if it had already come. I enter room No. 9 at the auction gallery. The auctioneer is selling a collection of pictures as I go in. "400 francs for 'The Pink Shrimps,' 450! 500! Come, gentlemen, it is worth more than that!" No one says anything. "Gone! 'The Pink Shrimps' by Vincent Van Gogh."

*
*   *

At 17 degrees of latitude, South, there are generals, counselors, judges, officials, gendarmes and a governor, as well as elsewhere. All the élite of society. And the governor says: "You see, my friends, there's nothing to do in this country but to pick up nuggets."

A fat attorney, the public prosecutor, after having examined two young thieves, makes me a visit. In my hut there are all sorts of odds and ends that appear extraordinary because here they are unusual: Japanese prints, photographs of pictures, Manet, Puvis de Chavannes, Dégas, Rembrandt, Raphael, Michael Angelo.

The fat prosecutor, an amateur who, they say, makes very pretty pencil sketches himself, looks about and before a portrait of Holbein's wife, from the Dresden Gallery, says to me: "That's from a piece of sculpture, isn't it?"

"No, it's a picture by Holbein, German school."

"Oh, well, it's all the same thing. I don't dislike that. It's pretty."

Holbein! pretty!

His carriage is waiting for him and he is going further on to lunch prettily on the grass, in sight of Orofena, surrounded by a pretty countryside.

The curé too (a member of the educated class) surprises me as I am painting a landscape.

"Ah, Monsieur, you are getting a fine perspective there"!!!

Rossini used to say: "*Je sais bien que ze ne souis pas un Bach, mais ze sais aussi que ze ne souis pas un Offenbach.*"

*
*   *

They say I am the champion billiard-player, and I am French. The Americans are furious and propose that I should play a match in America. I accept. Enormous sums are wagered.

I take the steamer for New York; there is a frightful storm, all the passengers are terrified. After a perfect dinner I yawn and go to sleep.

In a great luxurious room (American luxury) the famous match takes place. My opponent plays first. He scores a hundred and fifty. America rejoices.

I play, tock, tick, tock, just like that, slowly, evenly. America despairs. Suddenly a brisk fusillade of shots deafens the room. My heart does not leap; still slowly, evenly, the balls zig-zag, tock, tick, tock. Two hundred, three hundred.

America is beaten.

And I still yawn; slowly, evenly, the balls zig-zag, tock, tick, tock.

They say I am happy. Perhaps.

*

*　　　　　*

The great royal tiger is alone with me in his cage; nonchalantly he demands a caress, showing by movements of his beard and claws that he likes caresses. He loves me. I dare not strike him; I am afraid and he abuses my fear. In spite of myself I have to endure his disdain.

At night my wife seeks my caresses. She knows I am afraid of her and she abuses my fear. Both of us, wild creatures ourselves, lead a life full of fear and bravado, joy and grief, strength and weakness. At night, by the light of the oil-lamps, half suffocated by the animal stenches, we watch the stupid, cowardly crowd, ever hungry for death and carnage, curious at the shameful spectacle of chains and slavery, of the whip and the prod, never satiated of the howls of the creatures that endure them.

At my left, the quarters of the trained animals. The orchestra, about to begin, bursts into harsh and discordant sounds. Two poor men, the lords of creation, give each other fisticuffs and kicks. The trained·monkeys would not care to imitate them.

An image of life and society!

Along converging paths, rustic figures, empty of thought, seek for I know not what.

This looks like Pissarro.

A well by the seashore: some Parisian figures in gaily striped costumes, thirsty with ambition, doubtless seeking in this dry well the water that will slake their thirst. The whole thing confetti.

This looks like Signac.

Lovely colours exist, without our suspecting them, and may be divined behind the veil which modesty has drawn. Young girls, conceived in love, with hands that clasp and caress, invoking tender thoughts.

Without hesitation I say, by Carrière.

Ripe grapes overflow the edges of a shallow dish: on the cloth bright green and violet-red apples are mingled. The whites are blue and the blues are white. A devil of a painter, this Cézanne!

Once as he was crossing the Pont des Arts he met a comrade who had become famous.

"Hello, Cézanne, where are you going?"

"As you see, I'm going to Montmartre and you're going to the Institute."

A young Hungarian told me that he was a pupil of Bonnat's.

"My congratulations," I replied. "Your master has just won the prize in the postage stamp competition with his Salon picture."

The compliment went its way; you may imagine whether Bonnat was pleased. The next day the young Hungarian was ready to fight me.

*
*   *

THE CLOISONNÉ VASES

Far away, over there, the Nipponese countryside is covered with snow; the peasants are all in their houses.

To save you from entering by the chimney, for the doors are all closed, I shall introduce you by the sole means of a story into the midst of a Nipponese family who are peasants for nine months of the year and artists for the three months of winter. What you have seen in one house will tell you about them all; for they are all alike, animated with the same life, the same labours, especially the same gaiety. The interior is everything at once, a little factory, a sleeping-chamber, a refectory, etc., but it scarcely recalls the little box our great, great academician, Pierre Loti, so well describes.

Nor will you find little Chrysanthemum, the sister of Rarahu, the Tahitian maiden, who were both so incapable of understanding the distinguished heart of an effete and blasé young man. The Japanese young man is effete too, but he is not yet disillusioned. Furthermore, he has no brother Yves by his side to whom he can unbosom himself.

In a Japanese household everything is simple and composed, nature and the imagination alike. They work and they live on fruit, and nature there is rich in fruits. You know all this well enough, Loti, but one must know how to taste it, to forget that one is an officer. The devil take it, one doesn't sleep with one's epaulets on!

Ah! what a fine fragrance tea has when you drink it from a cup you have made yourself and decorated so freely! And these adorable little baskets that everyone makes for gathering cherries when the fine weather has come back again. Woven by skilful fingers; the Japanese arabesques give them a stamp all their own.

And these marvelous cloisonné vases that demand so much patient application and taste. Every Japanese peasant manufactures his own vase to put his flowers in when the spring comes round. Peasant! except for the lettered class, the countryfolk and the townsfolk are all the same.

Would you like to take part in the operation? For them it will be a matter of two or three months, for you and me only a few minutes. I shall not put your patience to the proof with a long account (the story would fill pages). Publishers do not like this when the book is not going to bring in thousand-franc notes.

Besides, this is not a book; it is nothing but idle chatter.

First of all, the Nipponese peasant carefully makes his design and his composition on a bit of paper which, when it is rolled out, has the same extent of surface as the vase. He knows how to draw, not exactly as we do from nature; but every child is taught at school a general schema established according to the masters. Birds flying or at rest, houses, trees, everything in nature, in short, has an invariable form which the child quickly gets at his finger-tips. Composition alone is not taught him, and every encouragement is given to the roving imagination.

So here is our Nipponese householder installed with a copper vase before him, his design in plain sight beside him.

Pincers, shears, flattened copper wire: so much for his stock of tools. With great dexterity and exactness he gives his copper wire, placed on the surface of the vase, all the forms of the design that is before him; then by means of borax he solders all these outlines on the copper, placing them, of course, so as to correspond with the design on the paper. This operation completed, not without extreme care and the greatest skill, the filling in of all these empty spaces with ceramic pastes of different colours is nothing but child's play. Yet it requires reflection and a very special sense for the infinite varieties of harmony, no regard being paid to complementary colours.

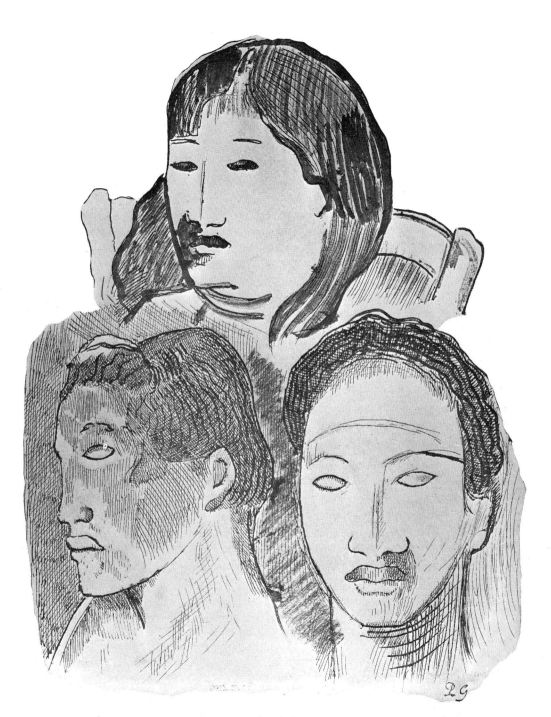

NOT DEVOID OF FEELING

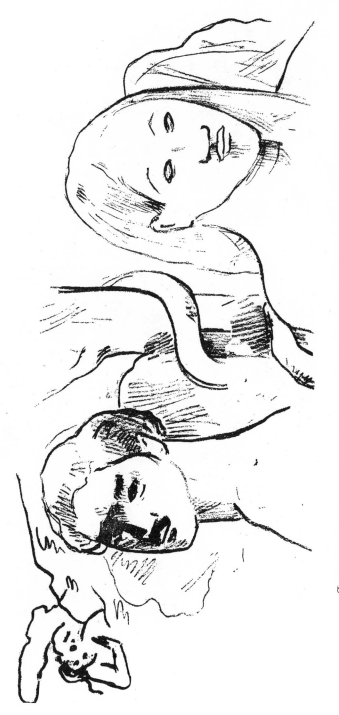

SKETCHES OF ALL SORTS, RANDOM VENTURES OF MY PEN AND MY IMAGINATION, STRAY FAN-
CIES. BUT THIS IS NOT AN ILLUSTRATION. WHY SHOULD IT BE AN ILLUSTRATION? HAVEN'T
YOU PHOTOGRAPHS? BUT THIS IS NOT SERIOUS. YOU ARE MISTAKEN; IT IS AS SERIOUS AS
POSSIBLE; ALL THAT REMAINS IS THE EXECUTION. THE INSTRUMENTS COME AFTERWARD.
Notes of the Author.

The artist, having finished his work of art, turns into a skilful potter. Nothing remains but to bake his vase. The oven of fire-proof earth can be bought from any merchant; the peasants always have them in different sizes. There is a little door cut in it for putting in and taking out the heat-indicator. Now the women and children enter the lists; they surround the oven and its contents with charcoal which they light slowly, very slowly. Each one, with a fan, blows on the fire in turn, and there are some innocent amusements. His reverence the priest does not like these Nohs, which are without words and consist entirely of gestures, a pastime in which they all excel.

The pledges are trinkets and combs, quickly offered and quickly lost. They grow warm, the fan becomes more and more active; the infernal work is nearing completion in the retort. Songs and laughter accompany this sham revel. Soon there is nothing left to forfeit and the combatants end by being as beautifully naked as when they were born. Not so much as a vine-leaf! Having nothing left to give they give themselves, and I assure you that neither the notary nor his honour the mayor regularizes these loves of the moment that could not be eternal.

It is late and everything is cooling off, slowly, very slowly, the young people and the terrible oven. Rest follows work well done.

In the morning all is calm, and on one of those little Japanese chests, inlaid with mother-of-pearl, the vase makes its first appearance. It is not yet finished, but already they want to enjoy a glimpse of it. Stepping far back, coming up close to it, the artist examines his work.

If he scolds, the children find the vase very ugly; if he is in a good humour and gives them sugar-plums, the smallest, the baby, says "Yes," and is silent. The eldest is full of admiration and says, "Papa, how beautiful it is!" Of course he says this in Japanese.

To finish the vase, he works every day, polishing it carefully.

And in the spring they go out in couples, gay and happy, wandering through the flowering woods where, amid aphrodisiacal perfumes, the senses regain their vigour. They pluck the bouquets that will go so well in the cloisonné vases!

P. S. I once related this to someone whom I thought intelligent. When I had finished he said to me, "But your Japanese are vulgar pigs!"

Yes, but in the pig all is good.

*

*   *

In this connection Remy de Gourmont said (in the *Mercure*): "It is truly a spectacle unique in history, this furious preoccupation with sexual morality which, under our indifferent eyes, destroys the sensibility of so many kindly men and so many amiable women."

*

*   *

Baby Jew goes to the Tuileries to play. His nurse takes him.

Baby Jew is very tired of playing with his red balloon.

Baby Jew notices a little Christian who is also very tired of playing with his superb wooden horse. He approaches and, looking disdainfully at the wooden horse, says, "Very ugly, your hobby-horse." Then with shrieks of joy he plays with his balloon.

Baby Christian weeps; then sighing timidly he says, "Do you want to exchange?"

Baby Jew returns triumphantly home with the wooden horse. And his father exclaims, "My love of a child! He's exactly like me! He'll go far!"

*

*   *

Do not advise or scold anyone who has come to ask a favour of you, especially if you don't do it for him.

Take care not to step on the foot of a learned idiot. His bite is incurable.

*

*   *

It was in the days of Tamerlane, I think in the year X, before or after Christ. What does it matter? Precision often destroys a dream, takes all the life out of a fable. Over there, in the direction of the rising sun, for which reason that country is called the Levant, some young men with swarthy skins, but whose hair was long, contrary to the custom of the soldier-like crowd, and thus indicated their future profession, found themselves gathered together in a fragrant grove.

They were listening, whether respectfully or not I do not know, to Vehbi-Zunbul Zadi, the painter and giver of precepts. If you are curious to know what this artist could have said in these barbarous times, Listen.

Said he: "Always use colours of the same origin. Indigo makes the

26

best base; it turns yellow when it is treated with spirit of nitre and red in vinegar. The druggists always have it. Keep to these three colours; with patience you will then know how to compose all the shades. Let the background of your paper lighten your colours and supply the white, but never leave it absolutely bare. Linen and flesh can only be painted by one who knows the secret of the art. Who tells you that flesh is light vermilion and that linen has grey shadows? Place a white cloth by the side of a cabbage or a bunch of roses and see if it will be tinged with grey.

"Discard black and that mixture of white and black they call grey. Nothing is black and nothing is grey. What seems grey is a composite of pale tints which an experienced eye perceives. The painter has not before him the same task as the mason, that of building a house, compass and rule in hand, according to the plan furnished by the architect. It is well for young men to have a model, but let them draw the curtain over it while they are painting. It is better to paint from memory, for thus your work will be your own; your sensation, your intelligence, and your soul will triumph over the eye of the amateur. When you want to count the hairs on a donkey, discover how many he has on each ear and determine the place of each, you go to the stable.

"Who tells you that you ought to seek contrast in colours?

"What is sweeter to an artist than to make perceptible in a bunch of roses the tint of each one? Although two flowers resemble each other, can they ever be leaf by leaf the same?

"Seek for harmony and not contrast, for what accords, not for what clashes. It is the eye of ignorance that assigns a fixed and unchangeable colour to every object; as I have said to you, beware of this stumbling-block. Practise painting an object in conjunction with, or shadowed by— that is to say, close to or half behind—other objects of similar or different colours. In this way you will please by your variety and your truthfulness—your own. Go from dark to light, from light to dark. The eye seeks to refresh itself through your work; give it food for enjoyment, not dejection. It is only the sign-painter who should copy the work of others. If you reproduce what another has done you are nothing but a maker of patchwork; you blunt your sensibility and immobilize your colouring. Let everything about you breathe the calm and peace of the soul. Also avoid motion in a pose. Each of your figures ought to be in a static position. When Oumra represented the death of Ocraï, he did not raise the sabre of the executioner, or give the Khakhan a threatening gesture, or twist the culprit's mother in convulsions. The sultan, seated on his throne, wrinkles his brow in a frown of anger; the executioner, standing, looks at Ocraï as on a victim who inspires him with pity; the mother, leaning against a pillar, reveals her hopeless grief in this giving way of her strength and her body. One can therefore without weariness spend an hour before this scene, so much more tragic in its calm than if, after the first moment had passed, attitudes impossible to maintain had made us smile with an amused scorn.

"Study the silhouette of every object; distinctness of outline is the attribute of the hand that is not enfeebled by any hesitation of the will.

"Why embellish things gratuitously and of set purpose? By this means the true flavour of each person, flower, man or tree disappears; everything is effaced in the same note of prettiness that nauseates the connoisseur. This does not mean that you must banish the graceful subject, but that it is preferable to render it just as you see it rather than to pour your colour and your design into the mould of a theory prepared in advance in your brain."

Some murmurs were heard in the grove; if the wind had not carried them off, one might perhaps have heard such evil-sounding words as Naturalist, Academician, and the like. But the wind made off with them while Mani knit his brows, called his pupils anarchists, and then continued:

"Do not finish your work too much. An impression is not sufficiently durable for its first freshness to survive a belated search for infinite detail; in this way you let the lava grow cool and turn boiling blood into a stone. Though it were a ruby, fling it far from you.

"I shall not tell you what brush you ought to prefer, what paper you should use, or in what position you should place yourself. This is the sort of thing that is asked by young girls with long hair and short wits who place our art on a level with that of embroidering slippers and making toothsome cakes."

Gravely Mani moved away.

Gaily the young men rushed away.

In the year X all this took place.

Contemporary judgments:

A petulant lady[1] (experienced, too experienced) said to my fiancée: "Of course, my child, you're marrying an honest fellow, but how *stupid* he is, how *stupid* he is!"

A little later a young painter, who had just got off the ship, said:

[1] A woman who had frightened me and whom I, being a Joseph, had not dared to understand.

"Gauguin, you know, is a rough sailor. He is quite clever at making little boats with their sails set, well put together. Perhaps So-and-so will polish him up."

There's something to save one from the sin of pride!

Still later, another precocious young man wrote: "An ardent pioneer, with my head full of ideas, I turned up the soil and found nothing. Seeing which Gauguin, who was cleverer than I, picked up all the treasures."

Concerning this seeker, a lover of art has said: "He traces a drawing, then he traces this tracing, and so on till the moment when, like the ostrich, with his head in the sand, he decides that it does not resemble the original any longer. Then!! he signs.

To avenge himself on Gauguin, this charming young man, who was supported by a credulous Mæcenas, wrote to a friend of Gauguin's: "My dear and tender friend, Gauguin has made you a cuckold."

To which the friend, justly convinced that it was a calumny, replied, "Guess again!"

And our charming young man, to avenge himself on this incredulous friend, who was also a painter, wrote on a letter addressed to him, "Monsieur Z, lessor of property." Seeing which, the friend wrote back, to Cairo, "Monsieur Zero, lessee."

This will teach you not to consort with the impudent.

But I do not store these things up. The road grows rougher and rougher; one grows old. The memory of evil vanishes in smoke. The velvet over one's consciousness hides the thorns and softens their sting.

Glory is a poor thing if it is so poorly constructed that it crumbles at the first breath. Besides, the real people avoid it. Solitude is so good, forgetfulness so restores our serenity when, conscious of sin, we desire deliverance even while we dread the unknown Hereafter.

"Giant, you are mortal." That is enough to humiliate one.

The problem one seeks to solve—easy at the beginning—a sphinx at death.

A handful of small coins thrown to the winds by a Croesus, of which, after a struggle, the strongest or the cleverest gathers up a trifling portion, glorying in his victory. His pride tumbles quickly enough when, with the little two-sous piece he has won with such difficulty, he tries to get something at the tobacconist's.

A neighbour of mine says, "Of course there is something in this gentleman's philosophy; if there is a good deal in it, so much the better; but as for me, who am only a fool, I say it comes to very little."

"He's a thoroughly honest fellow, heaven knows," said she, "but how stupid he is!!"

This is not a book.

*

*   *

Along the mulepath, both of them in blue with silver stripes, two brave fellows are swaying forward, for the curved line is certainly the shortest one; the Government wine loosens the limbs and thickens the tongue. It would be just as it is in the song if this were not in the Marquesas. Catching sight of a merry little golden face the police-sergeant exclaims, "She's mine!" To which the gendarme at once replies, "Sergeant, you're wrong there!"

And the merry little face also replies, without being in the least put out: "The first one pays two piastres, the second has to pay only one."

This time the gendarme, seeing that the little one is as matter-of-fact as if she were in Paris, replies, "Sergeant, you're right!"

"No, no, Monsieur le gendarme, you take the first shot—just like the English."

But a gendarme could not go ahead of his sergeant,—being in the Marquesas doesn't help matters. And these ladies know what they are about. The missionaries say to them, "Sin must have its excuse." The money is the excuse.

Reading the Journal des Voyages a man dreams of leaving Paris and a civilization that torments him; he takes the train and the boat at Marseilles, a sumptuous vessel.

Once on board and a few days out, he begins to know this Colonial world of which he has had no suspicion.

"Oh, the delights of living in a regiment under a ferule, with the security of the mess and the possible aureole of a palm!" (Remy de Gourmont).

Every day brilliant banquets, long tables of succulent dishes; an officer presides at each table.

"Steward! What's this? Do you think I'm accustomed to eating this sort of food? The government pays here and I want something for my money."

At home the clerk dines off two sous' worth of figs and one sou's worth of radishes. On Sunday, salad, with a sop of vinegar, flavoured with garlic. On shipboard it's different; one is on leave and when the government pays the bill we like to gobble and grumble at the same time.

Across the great ocean, a ship has just touched land, an islet unmarked on the map. There are three inhabitants, however, a governor, a sheriff's officer and a dealer in tobacco and postage stamps. Already!!!

Ah! readers, you think it would be pleasant to find a tranquil corner sheltered from evil people. Not even the island of Doctor Moreau, not even the planet Mars offers this, as we have just discovered since the Martians, to avenge the Boers, descended on London and started a panic among all those brave Englishmen.

When you reach Tahiti, the travellers who are going back get off the ship. The new arrivals must be inspected; the governor is there (the top-hat is indescribable) and all the riff-raff. Whispers. . . . At last, but very graciously, they ask, "Have you any money?"

But don't lose hope yet; evening comes, at last you are going to taste the forgetfulness of civilization. In the centre of the little square is a small kiosk just about big enough to hold all the members of the philharmonic society. The lamps once lighted, charming modern music delights you. Catching sight of a clerk wearing a cap who is distributing tickets for the merry-go-round, you forget yourself and ask for an omnibus ticket, Madeleine-Bastille. Still absent-minded, you take your seat in a little vehicle drawn by the wooden horses. It goes round, it goes round again. This isn't the Bastille. A mistake!! It's Tahiti!

*

*   *

I go into the café, No. 9 on the Boulevard. Everybody goes there, the beautiful Aryan race comes and goes. In the café, No. 9 on the Boulevard, I draw, I look about, I listen without finding much to attract me. The marble-topped tables in the café invite one's pencil. The ices draw the crowd, a promiscuous crowd; everybody is there. I draw promiscuously too. Everything is beautiful, everything is ugly.

Look! there is a head I know! Where the devil have I seen it? The profile is angular and I try to remember who it can be. Ah! I have it, it's myself! I resign myself without too much regret. I believed I was better looking. The Truth! At No. 9 Madame says, "What will you have? Champagne, I suppose?" And I modestly answer, "Give me a peppermint."

She, smartly dressed and with a heavy odour of verbena, takes a small glass of beer. Over there too the mirrors give back the faces of men and women; they are not beautiful. And I, sitting at the hetæra's side, remark to myself, "They say love beautifies." I try to let myself be convinced; my pencil refuses pitilessly. The Truth!!

*

*　　　*

Often, very often, the negro, the mulatto, the quadroon runs the government in a Colony where he was not born. Often educated, even intelligent, they still remain negroes, mulattos, quadroons. The Gallic cock, the former master, becomes the slave and no longer crows, cock-a-doodle-doo, as he formerly did. In his place, the Ethiopian crow becomes the master and croaks, *Allons, enfants de la Pat'ie, le jou' de gloi'e é pa'mi nous. . . !!*

During my stay in Martinique a negro, mulatto, quadroon, fell into a dispute with a man from Bordeaux and insults followed. The man from Bordeaux demanded a duel, which was accepted by our negro, mulatto, etc., and a meeting was agreed upon in the sugar-cane. The negro witnesses passed round among both sides lucky-stones and pick-me-ups.

On the field our man from Bordeaux was seized with colic. Excusing himself for the accident, he went off into the sugar-cane to undo his trousers. The operation, we must suppose, took a long time, for the impatient witnesses came to the rescue.

"What!" said our man from Bordeaux, "hasn't the negro, mulatto . . . gone away yet? Tell him straight from me . . . if he waits there fifty years, for fifty years I'll go on having business here."

Men from Bordeaux do not like negroes, mulattos, quadroons.

*

*　　　*

A newspaper in Tahiti that was not political would not be respectable. Elections in Tahiti are like Picpus and the bear at Berne. And so (who would have thought it!) you see me becoming a Picpus, in order not to be obliged to become Swiss.

On one side a dirty priest, on the other a miserable Protestant named Parpaillot. Never, never in my life, not even when I made my first communion, was I so ardent a Catholic, and with good reason. You shall learn why.

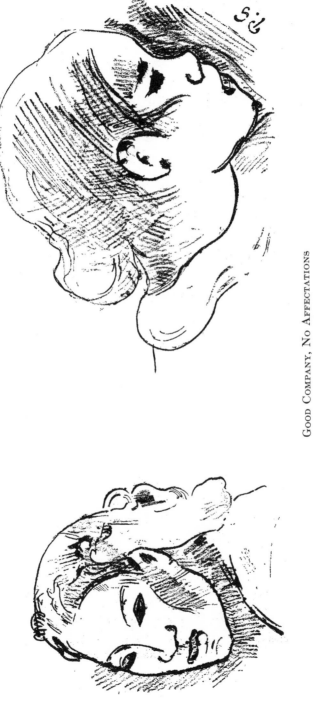

GOOD COMPANY, NO AFFECTATIONS

They are not Negresses, they are Maoris. The author has taken pains to tell their history in order to inform the critics.

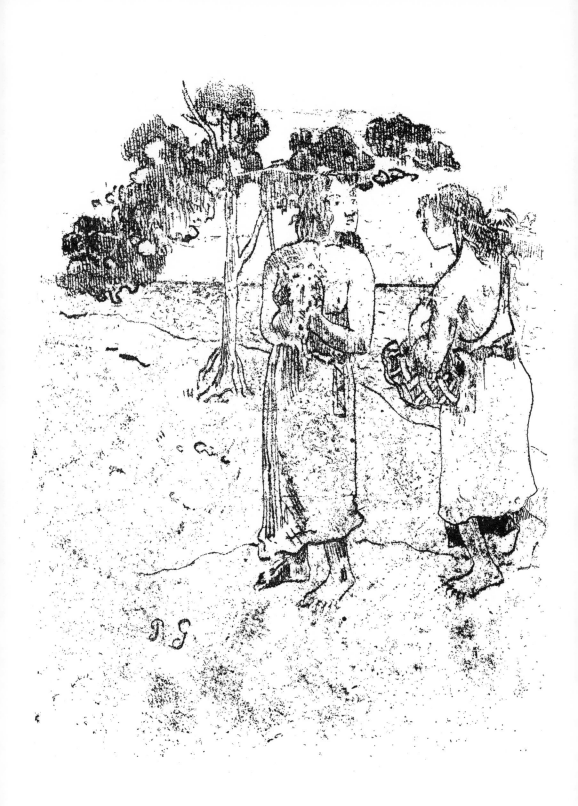

I had reached the point where I told myself it was time for me to set off for a simpler country where there were fewer officials. I was thinking of packing my trunks and going to the Marquesas, the Promised Land where there are more acres than one knows what to do with, food, game and a gendarme as gentle as a merino sheep to lead you about.

At once, my heart at ease, I took ship and arrived peacefully at Atuana, the chief town of Hivaoa.

It was quite necessary for me to come down a peg or two. The ant is not a lender, that is the least of its faults; and I had the air of a grasshopper that has sung all summer.

The first news that reached me on my arrival was that there was no land to be bought or sold, except at the mission. Even so, as the bishop was away, I should have to wait a month. My trunks and a shipment of building lumber waited on the beach. During this month, as you can well imagine, I went to mass every Sunday, forced as I was to play the rôle of a good Catholic and a railer against the Protestants. My reputation was made, and his reverence, without suspecting my hypocrisy, was quite willing (since it was I) to sell me a small plot of ground filled with pebbles and underbrush for the price of 650 francs. I set to work courageously and, thanks once more to some men recommended by the bishop, I was soon settled.

Hypocrisy has its good points.

When my hut was finished, I no longer thought of making war on the Protestant pastor, who was a well brought up young man with a liberal mind besides; nor did I think any longer of going to church.

A chicken had come along, and war had begun. When I say *a* chicken I am modest, for all the chickens arrived, and without any invitation.

His reverence is a regular goat, while I am a tough old cock and fairly well-seasoned. If I said the goat began it I should be telling the truth. To want to condemn me to a vow of chastity! That's a little too much; nothing like that, Lisette.

To cut two superb pieces of rose-wood and carve them after the Marquesan fashion was child's-play for me. One of them represented a horned devil (Père Paillard), the other a charming woman with flowers in her hair. It was enough to name her Thérèse for everyone without exception, even the school-children, to see in it an illusion to this celebrated love affair.

Even if this is all a myth, still it was not I who started it.

Good God, this is gossip for you! If ever I return to Paris I can at once offer myself as a concierge and read the feuilleton in the Petit Journal every morning. But then no conversation is possible here but gossip and filth. From his cradle, the child is up in everything—always the same thing, to speak correctly, like our daily bread.

It is not always exactly spiritual, but it's a rest, after the labours of art, to let one's mind play and one's body too. (The women are mercenary beyond a doubt.) Besides it preserves you from the boring austerity and the vile hypocrisy that make people so evil.

An orange and a side-glance, nothing more is necessary. The orange of which I speak varies from one to two francs; it is certainly not worth the trouble depriving oneself of it. You can easily be your own little Sardanapalus without ruining yourself.

No doubt the reader is looking for the idyll in all this, for there is no book without an idyll. But . . .

This is not a book.

To the native interpreter I said, "My boy, how do you say 'an idyll' in the Marquesan language?" And he answered, "What a funny person you are!" Pressing my investigations still further I asked him, "What is the word for Virtue?" And the good fellow answered, laughing, "Do you take me for an imbecile?"

The priest says this is all sin. The women, like astonished deer, seem to say with their velvety glances, "That's not true."

I know very well that back there in Paris, and in the provinces too, officials who are at home on leave are always telling wild stories. But don't believe a word of them; *here* the monsters are perfectly natural. They see clearly enough, without appearing to, that our clothes are ridiculous and that, although we boast of the contrary, we are just pretentious brutes.

"They promise," the women say, "and they do not keep their promises." Aside from this, they turn up their noses at us, as Colin does at Tampon.

If at Helder's or any other joint, you happen to run across a governor named Ed. Petit, look at him twice, for he is a damned ass.

Imagine it, years ago, when he was a purser on board the Hugon, he came to the Marquesas and made a number of marriages like Loti's. Being proud of one of them, he wanted to treat himself to the head of his mother-in-law, who was living a few feet underground in that charming island they call Taoata.

They scraped away and dug her up, and as the purser was for carrying off the famous head, the father-in-law cried, "How many piastres?"

"It's beyond price," replied our witty purser.

There is nothing more obstinate than a father-in-law who wants piastres, and the famous head was restored to its eternal domicile.

Like Hop-o'-my-Thumb, our purser inadvertently strews little stones along the path and at night makes off with the coveted head.

The missionary (a look-out man who lets nothing escape him) makes a written complaint, and the commander of the Hugon, thoroughly incensed, informs our purser that a mother-in-law is inviolable!

At his examinations at the École Coloniale, they asked him this question: "What is the proper way of balancing a budget?"

"That's quite simple, destroy it."

That extraordinary governor whom they call Ed. Petit wrote to the minister: "In the Marquesas, the race is disappearing day by day. Would it not be a good idea to send us the surplus from Martinique?"

This was written after the catastrophe of the eruption.

It is rather like that aide-de-camp who came to find the Emperor Napoleon I:

"Sire, a hundred thousand men are waiting for you below. Would it not be a good idea to bring them up by the little private stairway?"

And Napoleon I replied: "Tell them to come in, my good fellow."

If at Helder's or any other joint, or even at the Folies-Bergères, you run across Ed. Petit, tell him there is nobody like him.

*

*　　　　　*

God, whom I have so often offended, has spared me this time; at the moment when I am writing these lines a quite exceptional storm has just been making the most terrible ravages.

The day before yesterday, in the afternoon, the bad weather, which had been gathering for several days, took on threatening proportions. By eight in the evening it was a tempest. Alone in my hut, I expected each instant to see it collapse. The enormous trees which, in the tropics, have few roots, and those in a soil that has no resistance when it is once wet, were cracking on all sides and falling to the ground with a heavy thud.

Especially the *minores* (the breadfruit trees) the wood of which is very brittle. The gusts shook the light roofing of cocoa-tree leaves and, rushing in from all sides, prevented me from keeping the lamp burning. My house demolished, with all my drawings and the materials I had collected for twenty years; that would have been the ruin of me.

Toward ten o'clock a continuous noise, like the crumbling of a stone building, caught my attention. I could endure it no longer and went outside my hut. At once my feet were in water. By the pale light of the moon, which had just risen, I could see that I was in the midst of nothing more nor less than a torrent which, sweeping the pebbles along with it, was dashing against the wooden pillars of my house. There was nothing for me to do but to await the decision of Providence and resign myself.

The night was long. The moment dawn broke I stuck my nose outside. What a strange spectacle, this sheet of water, these granite rocks, these enormous trees come from heaven knows where! The road that runs in front of my land had been cut in two sections. Thanks to this I found myself shut up on an island. The devil would have been better off in a holy water basin.

I must tell you that what they call the valley of Atuana is a gorge, which is very narrow in certain spots where the mountain forms a wall. At these points all the water of the upper plateaus comes down in an almost perpendicular torrent. The Administration, unintelligent as usual, has done just the opposite of what it should have done. Instead of facilitating the flow of the flood waters it has shut them off on all sides with piles of stones. Not only this, but along the banks, even in the middle of the stream, it has allowed trees to grow, which are naturally overthrown by the torrent and form so many instruments of destruction, sweeping everything before them on their way. The houses in these warm countries, where no one has any money, are lightly built and a mere nothing turns them upside down, so that they too become agents of destruction. Is common sense really so unimportant that people can trample on it so? Even now their only thought is for hastily stopping up the holes made by the torrent. As for bridges,—where is the money? The eternal question, Where is the money?

If they would only let us simple colonists manage our own affairs and put what money we have into useful works, instead of maintaining all these insolent, mediocre officials! They would see then what a little colony can become, I mean a little colony like this of the Marquesas.

36

My hut has resisted and slowly we shall try to repair the damage that has been done.

But when is the next flood coming??

*

*   *

The Journal des Voyages and the Geography of Élisée Reclus have given you an authoritative description of the Marquesas with their inaccessible coasts, their steeply sloping granite mountains. There is nothing I want to add of my own inventing; it would not be scientific.

I want to tell you about the Marquesans, which will be difficult enough today. There is nothing picturesque to get one's teeth into. Even the language nowadays is ruined by all the badly pronounced French words: *un cheval (chevalé), un verre (verra)*, etc.

We do not seem to suspect in Europe that there exists, both among the Maoris of New Zealand and the Marquesans, a very advanced decorative art. Our fine critics are mistaken when they take all this for a Papuan art.

In the Marquesan especially there is an unparalleled sense of decoration. Give him a subject even of the most ungainly geometrical forms and he will succeed in keeping the whole harmonious and in leaving no displeasing or incongruous empty spaces. The basis is the human body or the face, especially the face. One is astonished to find a face where one thought there was nothing but a strange geometric figure. Always the same thing, and yet never the same thing.

Today, even for gold, you can no longer find any of those beautiful objects in bone, rock, iron-wood which they used to make. The police have *stolen* it all and sold it to amateur collectors; yet the Administration has never for an instant dreamed of establishing a museum in Tahiti, as it could so easily do, for all this Oceanic art.

None of these people who consider themselves learned have ever for an instant suspected the value of the Marquesan artists. There is not the pettiest official's wife who would not exclaim at the sight of it, "It's horrible! It's savagery!" Savagery! Their mouths are full of it.

Dowdy from head to foot, with their superannuated finery, vulgar hips, tumble-down corsets, imitation jewelry, elbows that threaten you or look like sausages, they are enough to spoil any holiday in this country. But they are white,—and their stomachs stick out!

The population that is not white is really elegant. Our fine critic is very much mistaken when he says, disdainfully, "Negresses!"—unless it is I who am all wrong in the way I describe them, and draw them, too. One person says that they are Papuans, another that they are Negresses. It is enough to make me seriously doubt whether I am really an artist.

Loti! Thank heaven, he finds them charming!

Let us settle, for the moment, what in my opinion should be the designation of this race, and call it the Maori race—leaving it to someone else, later, someone more or less photographic, to describe and paint it with a more civilized and literal art.

I say "really elegant" deliberately. All the women make their own dresses and in weaving their hats and trimming them with ribbons they are a match for any milliner in Paris; they arrange bouquets with all the taste of the Boulevard de la Madeleine. Their pretty, unconstrained bodies undulate gracefully under the chemise of lace and muslin. From their sleeves come hands that are essentially aristocratic, and if their large, heavy, shoeless feet offend us for a time, afterward it is the shoes that offend us. Another thing in the Marquesas that revolts the prudes is that all these young girls smoke pipes, the calumet, no doubt, to those who see savagery in everything.

However this may be, in spite of everything and notwithstanding everything, the Maori woman, even if she wanted to, could not be dowdy or ridiculous, for she has within her that sense of decorative beauty which I have come to admire in the Marquesan art after studying it. But is there nothing but that? Isn't there anything in a pretty mouth which, when it smiles, reveals teeth that are just as pretty? These, negresses? Come! And this pretty breast with its rosy bud, so rebellious against the corset!

What distinguishes the Maori woman from all other women, and often makes one mistake her for a man, is the proportions of the body. A Diana of the chase, with large shoulders and narrow hips. However thin one of these women's arms may be, the bony structure is unobtrusive; it is supple and pretty in its lines. Have you ever noticed at a dance the young girls of the Occident, gloved to the elbow, their thin arms, their sharp, excessively sharp elbows—ugly, in one word—the forearm larger than the upper arm? I have intentionally said the women of the Occident, for the arm of the Maori woman is like that of all Oriental women, though larger. Have you also noticed at the theatre the legs of the dancers, those enormous thighs (just the thighs), the knee enormous and turned in? This probably comes from an exaggerated spreading at the joint of the femur.

In the Oriental and especially the Maori woman, the leg from hip to foot offers a pretty, straight line. The thigh is very heavy, but not wide, which makes it round and avoids that spreading which gives to so many women in our country the appearance of a pair of tongs.

Their skin, of course, is of a golden yellow, which is ugly in some of them; but is it as ugly as all that in the rest, especially when it is naked— and when it is to be had for almost nothing? One thing, however, annoys me in the Marquesans, and that is their exaggerated taste for perfumes. The shopkeepers sell them a frightful perfumery made of musk and pat-chouli. When they are gathered together in church, all these perfumes become insupportable. But here again the fault is with the Europeans.

As for lavender water, you will never smell this, for the native, to whom one is forbidden to sell a drop of alcohol, drinks it as soon as he can lay his hands on it.

To return to the Marquesan art. This art has disappeared, thanks to the missionaries. The missionaries have considered that sculpture and decoration were fetishism and offensive to the God of the Christians.

That is the whole story, and the unhappy people have yielded.

From its very cradle, the new generation sings the canticles in incomprehensible French, recites the catechism, and after that . . . Nothing . . . as you can understand.

If a young girl, having picked some flowers, artistically makes a pretty wreath and puts it on her head, his reverence flies into a rage!!

Soon the Marquesan will be incapable of climbing a cocoanut-tree, incapable of going up the mountain after the wild bananas that are so nourishing to him. The child who is kept in school, deprived of physical exercise, his body always clad (for the sake of decency) becomes delicate and incapable of enduring a night in the mountains. They are all beginning to wear shoes and their feet, which are tender now, cannot run over the rough paths and cross the torrents on stones. Thus we are witnessing the spectacle of the extinction of the race, a large part of which is tubercular, with barren loins and ovaries destroyed by mercury.

Seeing this leads me to think, or rather to dream, of the time when everything was absorbed, numb, prostrate in the slumber of the primordial, in germ.

Principles invisible, indeterminate, indistinguishable at that time, all in the first inertia of their virtuality, without a perceptible or perceiving act, without active or passive reality or cohesion, possessing only one evident characteristic, that of nature itself, entire, without life, without expression, in solution, reduced to vacuity, swallowed up in the immensity of space which, without any form and as it were empty and penetrated to its very depths by night and silence, must have been a nameless void: this was chaos, the primeval nothingness, not of the Being but of life, afterwards to be called the empire of death, when life, produced from it, returns to it.

And my dream, with the boldness of the unconscious, solves many questions that my understanding dares not approach. Suddenly I am on the earth, and in the midst of strange animals I see beings that might well be men, though they resemble us but slightly. Without fear I approach; they look at me vaguely, without surprise. Beside them a monkey would seem by far the superior.

Drawing a piece of money from my pocket I give it to one of them. It is the most intelligent thing I can think of to do at the moment. He grasps it, carries it to his mouth, then, without anger, throws it away. Has he thought? I dare not hope so.

Now and then raucous sounds issue from his throat as from a cavern.

And in my dream an angel with white wings comes smiling toward me, behind him an old man holding in his hand an hour-glass.

"Useless to question me," he says, "I understand your thought. You must know that these beings are men such as you were once, before God began to create you. Ask this old man to lead you later into Infinity, and you will see what God wishes to do with you and learn that you today are far from completion. What would the work of the Creator be if it were all done in a day? God never rests."

The old man vanishes and I, awakening, raising my eyes heavenward, see the angel with white wings mounting towards the stars. His long, fair hair leaves in the firmament as it were a trail of light.

*

*   *

Let me tell you of a *cliché* that exists here and irritates me extremely: "The Maoris come from Malaysia."

On the boats that circulate in the Pacific, and when you land at Tahiti, the officers, who always know all about it, will say to you: "Monsieur, the Maoris are an export from Malaysia."

"But what makes you think so?" you exclaim.

There is no reason, it is the *cliché*. Do not attempt to resist it, observant painter as you may be; they will overwhelm you.

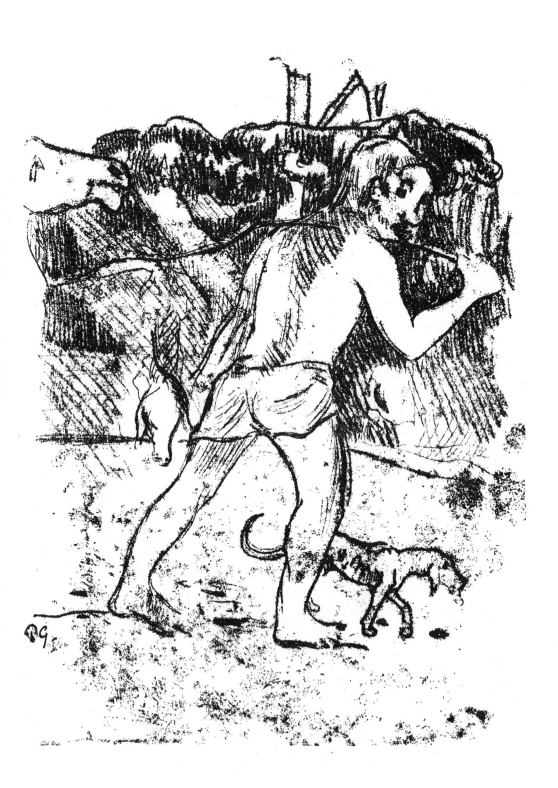

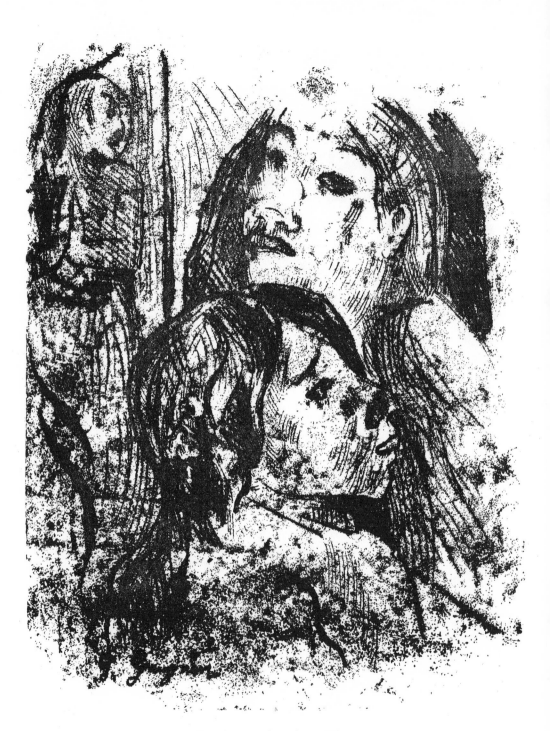

CONVERSATION WITHOUT WORDS

Of those who happen not to have heard this *cliché*, some say, "They are Papuans," and others, "They are Negroes."

In what epoch did the Deluge take place? The Bible alone has dared to make a positive statement.

From the loftiest mountains the waters receded; our beautiful France rose from the sea.

The waters of the other hemisphere submerged Oceania. Who cares? Only Malaysia has brought forth men. The ancient Oceanic land produce men? What an idea!

At what epoch did men begin to exist on our globe?

What does it matter, since I tell you that only Malaysia . . .

At what epoch did thought, freed from its animality, acquire some of its rudimentary elements, and in consequence make a beginning of language, the first component parts of which were the first sounds that came from the throat?

As one thinks of it, are there not grounds for supposing that the first forms of thought were identical, or almost identical, with the first forms of language? There is nothing extraordinary, then, in the fact that all the jackasses in the world should sing the same tune. There is nothing extraordinary in the fact that lately, quite lately, they should find in Malaysia, as well as in Oceania, in Africa, etc., the few generic words which the throat of the primitive being was able to utter, as well as the same mode of thinking. At the beginning, among all peoples, what man saw, touched and smelt formed his thoughts. Then came the desire to take, with its designation of the *I*, and the means of taking, the hand. Hence this word *rima* or *lima*, which means hand and which one finds in all tongues, in Malaysia as well as elsewhere, more or less transformed in pronunciation. Does not the Latin word *rama* resemble it? The same is true of the number 5, which represents a hand, and of 10, which represents two hands. Through all known time, the savages have used the spread arms for measuring, and the foot also.

As in "The Purloined Letter" of Edgar Poe, our modern intelligence, lost as it is in the details of analysis, cannot perceive what is too simple and too visible. As the Bible says, the mind of man mounts up to heaven and goes down again to the depths, but we cannot see so far down, and in spite of all our research we are unable to perceive the animals' mode of thinking, how the swallows, for example, contrive to return to the place of their birth. With their voices or with their tails the dogs express their feelings. We get out of the difficulty by means of the *cliché*, Instinct.

This question of language has been one of the principal causes of the adoption of the *cliché*—Malaysian-Maori.

It is better not to know than to know wrong.

And I shall maintain that for me the Maoris are not Malaysians, Papuans or Negroes.

*

* *

When you arrive in the Marquesas you say to yourself, seeing these tattooings that cover the face and the whole body: "These are terrible fellows. And they have been cannibals too."

You are altogether mistaken.

The native Marquesan is by no means a terrible fellow; on the contrary, he is an intelligent man and quite incapable of plotting evil. He is so gentle as to be almost foolish and he is timorous towards all in authority. People say he has been anthropophagous, imagining that this is ended, which is a mistake. He is so still, but without ferocity; he likes human flesh as a Russian likes caviare, as a cossack likes a tallow-candle. Ask a dozing old man whether he cares for human flesh; wide awake for once, his eyes shining, he will reply with infinite gentleness, "Oh, how good it is!"

Naturally there are a few exceptions; exceptional as they are, they inspire a great terror in all the others.

Apropos of old Père Orans, who died only a short time ago, I can tell you a story that may perhaps interest you. Père Orans the missionary, when he was young, was once gaily following a path that led to a district where he had some business, when he found that he was being trailed by a number of evil-looking fellows, the exceptions of which I have just spoken, who had decided that the missionary was just in the right condition to be eaten. They were preparing to carry out their plan when Père Orans, who had very sharp ears, suddenly turned round and with the greatest composure asked them what they wanted. One of them, very much frightened, enquired if he had any matches, so that he might light his pipe. The missionary drew from his pocket a large lens and set fire with it to the edge of his cassock. Astonished at the power of the white man, they bowed respectfully, but the lens became the property of the native.

Another story, this one much more recent.

A young American, fascinated no doubt by the women, left his ship and remained in the Marquesas. He established himself in a district of Hivaoa and, forced by necessity, tried to carry on a little trade.

One day he had the unfortunate idea of returning from Atuana with his sack of piastres fastened in plain sight to the pommel of his saddle. Night was coming on; he disappeared.

Suspicion fell immediately upon a Chinaman; the gendarme—a bad lot, as they all are—said he was the one, and this sufficed. It was not till three months later, that is to say, till three mails had come, that the Court returned to Papeete with the Chinaman and several witnesses. Naturally the Chinaman was acquitted on the spot.

This word "naturally" calls for an explanation. It is the rule in the Marquesas, when a crime occurs. The gendarme makes his enquiry, with his head in the sand and always on the wrong track, in spite of the information given him by the intelligent men in the neighbourhood. The police magistrate arrives long after, and his opinion at once becomes the same as that of the gendarme. Too much thoroughness is undesirable in the Marquesas.

The natives are accustomed to base their conduct on the terror inspired in them by evil-doers. Any individual who did not conform to this rule would at once be condemned to death. When a crime has been committed, everyone knows about it; but face to face with the Court no one knows anything.

The witnesses entangle the question in obscurities. Their language— always badly interpreted—gives them every facility to do this. They are able, with remarkable intelligence and imperturbable composure, to smooth over all the contradictions.

"But why did you say one thing a moment ago and just the contrary now?"

"It is because the Court frightens me, and when I am frightened I do not know what I am saying."

If there are two of them they accuse each other reciprocally, and each invariably answers: "I accuse the other man, because otherwise the judge will say it is I."

I remember this bit of naivety on the part of a presiding judge at the Court at Papeete:

"Interpreter, tell this man that he answers all my questions very intelligently. Is it because he had thought of all my questions before hearing them?"

Answer: "This man says he does not know why he should be asked this and that he replies as well as he can."

To return to our Chinaman. It was clear to everyone who reflected and knew the customs of the natives that this Chinaman could not have committed his crime alone and especially caused the body to disappear, in spite of the proximity of the sea. A Chinaman is too intelligent for that, for he knows (perhaps the Maori gods watch over everything that happens) that nothing can be done without the natives knowing of it, and that in consequence he, a foreigner, would be immediately denounced.

It was clear, therefore, that the Chinaman had accomplices, especially as the lover of one of his daughters was known to be one of the evil and criminal exceptions. But the police-sergeant would not listen to anything.

This is what had occurred, according to the information that was given to me as it was given to everybody. They all agree except on one point,—the hour and the place at which the crime was committed. There are different versions of this, but I suspect that they are deliberate contradictions.

As soon as he arrived in the district near his hut, the famous sack of piastres was observed, and our young American, vigorous and resolute, confident as young men generally are, took no pains to conceal it.

Our young American was killed by a vigorous blow of a stick on the neck, just as the guillotine would have done it. There were two of them, the Chinaman and his son-in-law. They proceeded to fight over the division of the piastres.

Then, later, the son-in-law and two other natives gave themselves up to their gluttony. The American was eaten.

I am passing over a good many details that have no importance in this narrative.

Here the reader will ask me a question to which I shall reply at once.

Why, now that all these facts are known, should they not again take up the charge against the accomplices?

Because there would be an immediate silence, and all this well vouched for gossip would turn into a fable, invented to amuse the credulous European.

The native Marquesan tongue is far from rich, as we know. The result is that the native trains himself in the skilful use of paraphrase. Thus, for example, when the gendarmes appear, evidently in search of information, they go on talking without any sign of embarrassment. One of them says: "I think the moon is going to be very bright, so that we are not going to catch any fish." This means: "We must be on our guard and keep things dark; we must beware of the brightness of the moon."

The Europeans can make nothing of it, and even if they could they would not be sure.

*
*   *

In Oceania a woman says: "I don't know whether I love him, for I haven't slept with him yet." Possession gives title.

In Europe a woman says: "I used to love him; since I have slept with him I don't love him any longer." Or: "I only love him when he is with me."

If even ten minutes before her marriage a woman is unwilling to give herself, you may be sure she is selling herself.

But she lacks confidence? Then it is your turn to lack confidence.

A rich woman got herself a child by her servant; still another man who deserts his child! Poor woman! Is it as bad as all that? But the servant says that it is he who has been deserted!

A foolish woman says she does not want to marry because she wants to have her child all to herself. The egoism of maternal love.

It is easy to say, "This is mine." But how much it costs to say, "This is ours."

Q. "What! you saw someone drowning and did not help him?"

A. "But he did not ask me to."

Maxims!! They are not practicable, they are meant for conversation and to give someone a chance to say, "Hello, there is a philosopher!"

To know how to give—that is a very good thing.
To know how to receive—that is still better.
Ah! the vanity of money! . . .
To have will is to will to have it.

They say, "Like father, like son." Children are not responsible for the faults of their fathers. I haven't a sou; that is my father's fault.

The song says, "If my father is a cuckold, it is because my mother wished it so."

There are some of these moral sayings that manage to avoid having any morals.

Just for a moment let me tell you something about Brittany. From Oceania to Brittany is not far when one is feeling calm and has one's pen in hand; one's fancy wanders. Why not? Besides, nothing happens by chance.

A newspaper I am glancing over tells me of certain men with Déroulède who have just discovered what real, patriotic republicanism is. Among them is a certain name that brings back to me a dreary individual we used to know at Pont-Aven. It is indeed the very same Marcel H.

This very distinguished looking gentleman would tap his wife on the shoulder as much as to say to us, "There's a fine piece of meat for you!" In fact, she was meat, nothing but meat.

And his little human pig's eye would add, "This meat is mine, mine alone."

During the first week he went regularly to meet the coach that brought the mail and asked, "Is there a package for me?"

We all became very curious and wondered what this package could be. The famous package arrived.

From the next morning on, we would see our Marcel H. installed by the river that winds about the property of David the miller, a great canvas before him on the easel and further off, on a superb boulder, the famous package, an immense stuffed swan. Our gentleman was making his picture for the next Salon (a Leda).

The fine piece of meat, whom we knew, had been painted in—but without a head—in Paris. Nothing remained but to paint the swan.

Seated beside him, but clothed and with her head on, the fine piece of meat knitted a pair of stockings.

"For the swan's white," he said, "I use only white zinc; for the fine piece of meat I use bitumen lake."

At the table d'hôte, addressing the man who was sitting next to him, an impressionist painter, he said: "Manet, you know, makes a rough sketch every day and when he finds one that suits him he sends it to the Salon. And then it's just made out of whole cloth."

When the month of September arrived, he said: "I am obliged to go back to Paris, for this is the time when my dealer arrives; he exports pictures to the Guano Islands."

Japanese sketches, prints of Hokusai, lithographs of Daumier, cruel observations of Forain—gathered together in an album, not by chance but by my own deliberate will. Among them I am enjoying the photograph of a painting by Giotto. Because they appear so very different I want to demonstrate their bonds of relationship.

In this warrior of Hokusai, Raphael's St. Michael has become Japanese. In another drawing of his, he and Michael Angelo meet. Michael Angelo (the great caricaturist!) shakes hands with Rembrandt.

Hokusai draws freely. To draw freely is not to lie to oneself.

In this little exhibition Giotto plays the chief part.

The Magdalen and her company arrive at Marseilles in a bark, if a section of a calabash can represent a bark. Angels precede them with their wings spread. No possible relation can be established between these persons and the tiny tower into which equally tiny men are making their entrance.

These personages in the bark, who look as if they were cut out of wood, immense as they are, must be very light since the bark does not sink. Meanwhile, in the foreground a draped figure, very much smaller, maintains itself in a most improbable fashion on a rock, one does not know by what marvelous law of equilibrium.

Before this canvas I have seen Him, always the same He, the modern man, who reasons out his emotions as he reasons the laws of nature, smiling that smile of the satisfied man and saying to me, "You understand that?"

Certainly, in this picture, the laws of beauty do not reside in the verities of nature. Look elsewhere. In this marvelous canvas one cannot deny an immense fecundity of conception. What does it matter whether the conception is natural or unlike nature? In it I see a tenderness and a love that are altogether divine. I should like to pass my life in such honest company.

Giotto had some very ugly children. Someone having asked him why he made such lovely faces in his paintings and such ugly children in his life, he answered, "My children are night work. . . . My pictures are my day work."

Did Giotto understand the laws of perspective? I have no desire to know. The processes which gave birth to his work are his, not mine; let us consider ourselves happy if we can enjoy his work.

With the masters I converse; their example fortifies me. When I am tempted to sin, I blush before them.

Three caricaturists:
  Gavarni jests elegantly.
  Daumier sculptures irony.
  Forain distils vengeance.

Three kinds of love: moral love, physical love, manual love. Morality, Debauchery, Prudence!

To a man who has not succeeded we say, "You made a mistake."
To one who has lost at the lottery, "You had bad luck."

When you are twenty two things are very hard to do: to choose a career, to choose a wife. All careers are good, but one cannot say, "All women are good."

Anomalies.—Of all the animals, man is certainly the least logical, the one that knows the least what he wants to do and the one that commits the most follies. Why is this so unless it is because he knows best how to reason? This should give us some food for reflection on the importance of reasoning and education.

Without being a Buffon, one ought to be able to make a few observations. Every day, at meal times, not a few cats invite themselves to my table and I regularly do them honour with plenty of rice and sauce.

They are all nearly wild. They want their dole without any caresses except glances. One female cat, the only one which is civilized enough for me to be unable to go out on the road without her following at my heels, is ferocious in every way, egoistical, jealous. The only one that growls while she eats. They are all afraid of her, even the males, unless she happens to take a fancy to one of them. But even then she bites and claws. The male submits to the blows, bowing before this female who plays the master's part so well.

All trained animals become stupid, hardly knowing how to find their own food for themselves, incapable of hunting for the medicaments that heal them. Dogs that end by having bad digestions are guilty of indecencies, knowing it but not suspecting that they smell badly.

I once happened to be in the roads at Rio de Janeiro. I was a pilot's apprentice. The heat was extreme; everyone was asleep on deck, some forward, some aft. The sleeping cabin-boy was dreaming too violently, and, also too violently, he fell into the water. "Man overboard!" Everyone woke up and stared stupidly at the boy, who was being swept along by the current toward the stern of the ship. A negro sailor cried out, "Thundering Jesus, he's going to drown!" Then, without a thought, he

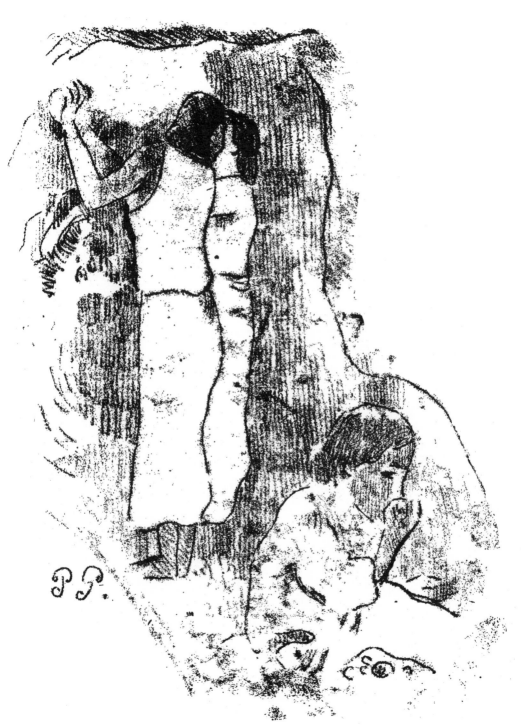

EATING

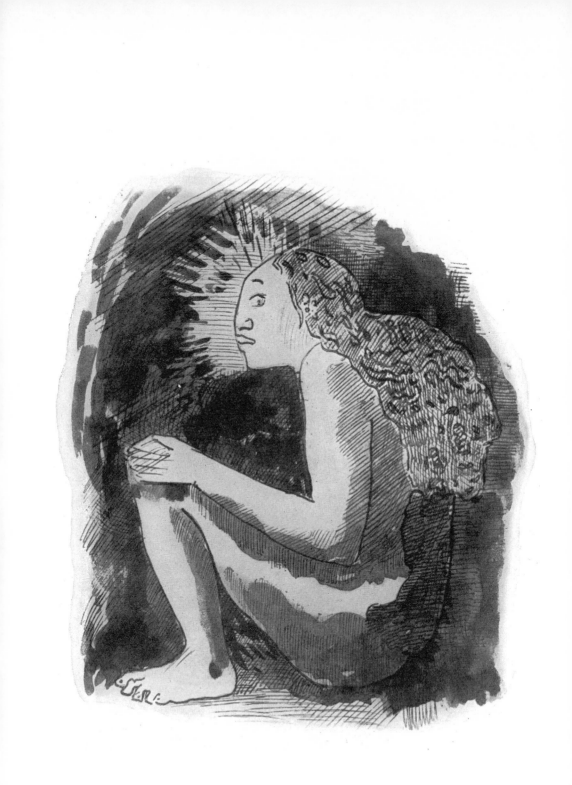

flung himself into the sea and brought the little cabin-boy to the ladder at the stern.

Beware of these pure souls, and if you make anyone a cuckold, do not keep your eye on the husband but on your own purse.

Intentionally, rather with malice prepense than from instinct, I write a bit smuttily here and there. It is because I want to prevent this miscellany from being read by prudes, those insupportable prudes who do not know how to dress themselves except in a livery.

"You understand, my friend, that I can't take my lawful wife to those receptions of yours where your mistress appears."

When Madame is present (she is an honest woman because she is married) everyone is on his best behaviour. When the party is over and they all go home, our honest Madame, who has yawned the whole evening, stops yawning and says to her husband, "Let's have some nice piggy talk before we do it." And the husband says, "Let's not do anything but talk. I have eaten too much this evening."

A virginal young woman, who has brilliantly passed her doctorate in medicine, dares not specialize in the secret diseases and speaks of Master John Henry with a blush.

Apropos of Master John, it is worth noting that today, when it is the fashion to send pure young girls to study painting in the ateliers with the men, all these virgins draw the nude male model with the greatest care, Master John with more accuracy than the face. When they leave the atelier, these young virgins, foreigners for the most part and always respectable, their modest eyes slightly lowered, glancing through their lashes, go to Lesbia to console themselves. A curious anomaly.

I remember one of them, a very pretty Scotch girl. She used to take her meals at a little creamery frequented by the artists. One fine day, an insipid young Belgian girl, whose flat corset looked like a breast-plate, happened to drop in. Our Scotch girl came and sat down beside her, and with a good deal of simpering questioned her about her arrival in Paris, what she was planning to do, and whether they were going to have the pleasure of seeing her at the atelier. And with her eyes very excited, her cheeks highly coloured, she added, "Come and see me." The breast-plated Belgian answered dryly, "Thank you." How the famous Minna did laugh at this!!

The great scholar, the famous misogynist, trembled before *her*. There are misogynists who are misogynists because they love women too well, and tremble before them.   .   .   .

I love women, too, as you know, when they are fat and vicious; but I am not a misogynist and I do not tremble before them. My only fear, in such cases, is that I may not have a penny in my pocket. Why should I care for this one rather than another? Unfortunately, it is I and not the women who say, "Nothing doing." As long as the brain is strong, what does Master John Henry matter?

Letter of Paul Louis Courier:

"You should think, Madame, of what I told you yesterday, and con sider me a little. I am willing that the thing itself should be indifferent to you, but the pleasure of giving pleasure, is that nothing? Come, between ourselves, I know it makes you neither hot nor cold, brings you neither good nor harm, pleasure nor pain; but that is a fine reason for saying no when you are entreated! Fie! are you not ashamed to make one ask twice for things that cost so little, as Gaussin said, and for which, after all, you feel no repugnance?"

Another letter—a passage from it:

"Without perceiving me she opens the door, and with a step and a leap there I am inside with her. A lively dispute, a theatrical scene. She wishes to drive me away; I remain. She is in despair, I laugh: 'Pianse, prega, ma in vano ogni parola sparse.'

"Salvat might come, was coming indeed; it was the hour, the danger was increasing with each instant. Without any delicacy, without flowery language, I told her the price I set on my retreat. 'Dunque, fa presto,' said she. Presto. I did it and left. Henceforth, I could do with her as I wished, for she is at my discretion; I might even betray her. Good-for-nothings like you would be sure to do so. But as you know, I take no pains to imitate you. I see her, I speak to her as before: the same tone, the same manner," etc.   .   .   .

For shame, Monsieur Courier; I like the other letter better.

As for me, if a woman said to me, "Hurry up," or asked me for a hunpred sous more, it would be all off with me.

Catherine the Great, Catherine of Russia, had but one desire left; she wished there were a simple soldier, strong and handsome, amorous and bold enough to penetrate into her apartments and violate her.

Seeing this, her lover, her great favourite, went and found the handsomest man in the army and said to him: "Here is a little key that will open the door to Catherine's apartments. Go in and ravish her as roughly and violently as you can. If you do it you will be rewarded; if you don't, you will receive a hundred stripes with the knout."

Catherine enjoyed the greatest gratification.

One fine day, the favourite confessed his duplicity. He was killed (at Catherine's command). Is there anything strange in this? Was not the favourite barbarously stupid?

The author adds to his narrative this reflection: "Is it really permissible to call such a woman great?"

Stupid author! I should say she was great. And just because of this.

*
*   *

The Chinese are in a redoubt, protected by big, sharply pointed bamboos.

Their assailants, a French battalion, have not expected any such resistance and are obliged to withdraw, almost in a panic. The colour-sergeant, left alone, sticks his flag in the earth and, half dead with fear, hides among the bamboos.

The battalion returns to the offensive, seeing which our colour-sergeant, still at their head, arrives at the redoubt. Seeing which, also, the Government gives him the cross, the famous cross. Seeing which, also, everyone says: "He was a brave one, that fellow!"

*
*   *

One of the assistant masters at my school, Daddy Baudoin, was a grenadier who had survived from Waterloo. He was a great hand at colouring pipes. In the dormitory we used to lift our shirts and say disrespectfully, "Attention! Present arms!" And the old man, a tear in his eye, would begin thinking of the great Napoleon. The great Napoleon knew how to make them die, he also knew how to make them live. "There aren't any soldiers left," Daddy Baudoin would say. At our studies he was the child and we were the men. One of the boys said, "I am going to be a Mirabeau "; he became a Gambetta. I said, "I am going to be a Marat"! . . . Does anyone really know what he is going to become?

*

*   *

At Taravao, old Lucas says to his wife, "Lillia, be nice to the governor when he comes; our vacation depends on it."

And the delighted missionary proudly says, "It was we who got old Lucas married." There was not a pimp who would have her. This sentence was uttered by Manet when someone reproached him for having done a portrait of Pertinset. In all departments there are those who survive and those who go under.

*

*   *

For some time three whaling-ships have been in our waters, and the gendarmes are all on edge. Why this excitement, this sullen anger? "Whalers! . . . Whalers! . . ."

But what on earth does it all mean? Are the whalers bearers of bad luck? Do they bring the cholera with them or some whale-plague that will turn into a human plague? All I know is, the gendarmes say to me, "Monsieur, the whalers are a pest!"

"Let's go and have a look," one of them says. "Let's see what we can find out," says another. And they both begin telling tales. I shall tell you a tale too, but I shall tell you the right one.

Well, it is the custom of the whalers never to carry money with them. For they know quite well that money cannot be eaten at sea and that on land there are philosophers who despise the vile metal.

It is thus, imbued with these false ideas, that they come to the Marquesas, especially Taoata. They count on getting in their supply of water and exchanging their cheap wares and light flannel for bananas, meat and other provisions.

What an idea! Landing merchandise that has not paid duty!!

The natives, delighted to exchange the produce of the land which they do not need for things they enjoy, cannot make out whether we really want to do them good or harm. But there are three or four rag-tag and bob-tail dealers in codfish who cry out that it is "unpatriotic competition."

The result is that the gendarmes are all out of breath, while every night, from all directions, the ship is relieved of its merchandise. Well-stocked with provisions it sets out again. And the island of Taoata is the richer for a few European products. Where is the harm, and why all these outcries? When will man understand what Humanity means?

*
*   *

Various episodes, many reflections, a few whims have found their way into this miscellany, come no one knows whence, converging and separating, a child's game, the figures of a kaleidoscope. Serious sometimes, often droll, as frivolous nature wills it. Man, they say, trails his double after him. One remembers one's childhood; does one remember the future? Memory of the before—memory, perhaps, of the after? I do not know precisely. But when we say, "It will be fair tomorrow," are we not remembering the past, the experience that makes us think as we do?

I remember having lived. I also remember not having lived. No longer ago than last night I dreamed I was dead. Curiously enough this occurred at a time when I am truly living happily.

Waking dreams are almost the same thing as sleeping dreams. Sleeping dreams are often bolder, and sometimes a little more logical.

Let me go back to what I have already told you: this is not a book.

Besides, I believe that, like myself, you are all far less serious than you care to admit, and just as perverse, some being more intelligent, others less.

"We know that well enough," you will say. But it is a good thing to say it again, to say it unceasingly, all the time. Like the floods, morality overwhelms us, stifles liberty in the hatred of fraternity.

Breeches morality, religious morality, patriotic morality, the morality of the soldier, of the gendarme. . . . The duty of exercising one's function, the military code, Dreyfusard or non-Dreyfusard. The morality of Drumont, of Déroulède. The morality of public education, of the censorship. Aesthetic morality; the morality of criticism assuredly. The morality of the bench, etc.

My miscellany will change nothing of this but . . . it's a relief.

DEGAS

20 January, 1903.

Who knows Degas? No one—that would be an exaggeration—only a few. I mean, know him well. He is unknown, even by name, to the millions of readers of the daily papers. Only the painters, many because they are afraid of him, the rest because they respect him, admire Degas. Do they really understand him?

Degas was born . . . I don't know when, but it was so long ago that he is as old as Methuselah. I say Methuselah because I suppose that Methuselah at one hundred years must have been like a man of thirty in our days. Degas, in fact, is always young.

He respects Ingres, which means that he respects himself. In appearance, with his silk hat on his head, his blue spectacles over his eyes—not to forget the umbrella—he is the image of a notary, a bourgeois of the time of Louis-Philippe.

If there exists a man who cares little about looking like an artist, it is certainly he; he is so much of one. He detests all liveries, even this. He is as good as gold; yet, fine as he is, people think him morose.

A young critic who has a mania for issuing judgments, like an augur pronouncing a sentence, said once, "Degas is a good-natured old bear." Degas a bear!! He who in the street carries himself like an ambassador at court. Good-natured!! That is a trivial thing: he is something more than that.

Degas at one time had an old Dutch woman as a servant, a family relic who, in spite of this or perhaps because of it, was insupportable. She used to serve at table and Monsieur never talked. One day when the bells of Notre Dame de Lorette rang out deafeningly, she cried, "They would never ring like that for that Gambetta of yours!"

Ah! I know what they mean by "bear"; Degas defies the interviewer. The painters seek his approval, ask for his appreciation and he, the bear, the surly one, in order to escape saying what he thinks, says to you very pleasantly, "Do excuse me, but I çan't see clearly, my eyes . . ."

On the other hand, he doesn't wait until you are known. He has a power of divination with the young and he, who knows everything, never speaks of a defect of knowledge. To himself he says, "He will learn later," and to you he says, like a good papa, as he did to me at my début, "You have your foot in the stirrup."

No one who has power can annoy him.

I remember Manet, too, another whom no one annoyed. Once, seeing a picture of mine (at the beginning) he told me it was very good. I answered, out of respect for the master, "Oh, I am only an amateur!" At that time I was in business as a stockbroker, and I was studying art only at night and on holidays.

"Oh, no," said Manet, "there are no amateurs but those who make bad pictures." That was sweet to me.

Why is it that, today, as I look back over the past down to this very moment, I am obliged to see (it is obvious enough) that of all those whom I have known, especially the young men whom I have advised and helped, *there is hardly one who knows me any longer?*

I do not wish to understand it.

Yet I cannot say, with false modesty—

> Qu' as tu fait, O toi que voilà,
> Pleurant sans cesse,
> Dis, qu' as tu fait, toi que voilà,
> De ta jeunesse? (*Verlaine*)

For I have worked and spent my life well, intelligently, even courageously, without weeping, without tearing things,—and I have very good teeth.

Dégas has a contempt for theories of art, he has no interest in technique.

At my last exhibition at Durand-Ruel's (Works in Tahiti, '91–'92) there were two well-intentioned young men who could not understand my painting. As they were respectful friends of Degas', and wished to be enlightened, they asked him for his feeling about it.

With that good smile of his, paternal if he is so young, he recited to them the fable of the dog and the wolf: "You see Gauguin is the wolf."

So much for the man. What is the painter?

One of the earliest known· pictures of Degas is a cotton warehouse. Why describe it? It would be better for you to go and see it, to take a careful look at it, and especially not to come and tell us, "No one could paint cotton better." The cotton is not the point, nor even the men who are handling it. He himself knew this so well that he passed on—to other works. But already his defects (from the academic standpoint) had asserted themselves and left their stamp, and one could see that, young as he was, he was a master. A bear already! The tendernesses of intelligent hearts are not easily seen.

Brought up in a fashionable set, he yet dared to go into ecstasies before the milliners' shops in the Rue de la Paix, the charming laces, those famous touches by which our Parisian women drive you into buying an extravagant hat. And then to see them again at the races, smartly perched on the chignons, and below, or rather through it all, the tip of the sauciest of noses!

Then to go in the evening, as a rest after the day's work, to the opera!

There, Degas told himself, everything is false, the light, the scenery, the wigs of the dancers, their corsets, their smiles. Nothing is real but the effects they create, the skeleton, the human structure, the movement; arabesques of all sorts. What strength, suppleness and grace! At a certain moment, the male intervenes, with a series of *entrechats*, to support the swooning dancer. Yes, she swoons; but she swoons only at that moment. If you are aspiring to sleep with a dancer, do not permit yourself to hope, for a single moment, that she will swoon in your arms. That never happens; the dancer only swoons on the stage.

Degas' dancers are not women, they are machines moving with graceful lines and marvelous balance, arranged with all the pretty artificiality of the Rue de la Paix. The light gauzes float upward and it never occurs to you that you are seeing the under side of them,—there is nothing to blemish the whiteness.

The arms are too long, according to the gentleman who, with his yardstick in his hand, is so clever at calculating proportions. I know this too, so far as mere nature is concerned. Decoration is not landscape, it is decoration. De Nittis did the other thing, and much better.

The race-horses, the jockeys, in Degas' scenes are often enough sorry jades ridden by monkeys. There is no pattern in any of these things, only the life of the lines, lines, lines again. His style is himself.

Why does he sign his works? No one has less need to do so than he.

In these later days he has done a good many nudes. The critics, as a rule, see the woman. Degas sees the woman, too . . . but he is no more concerned with women than he used to be with dancers,—at most with certain phases of life learned through indiscretions.

What is he concerned with? Design was at its lowest ebb; it had to be restored; and looking at these nudes, I exclaim, "It is on its feet now!"

Man and painter, he is an example. Degas is one of those rare masters who, having only to stoop to take them, has disdained fortune, palms, honours, without bitterness, without jealousy. He passes through the crowd so simply. His old Dutch servant is dead, or she would say: "The bells would never ring like that for you."

One of those many painters who exhibit with the Independents in order to be called independent, said to Degas: "Aren't we going to have the pleasure, some day, of seeing you among us at the Independents?"

Degas smiled in his amiable way. . . . And you say he's a bear!

*

*   *

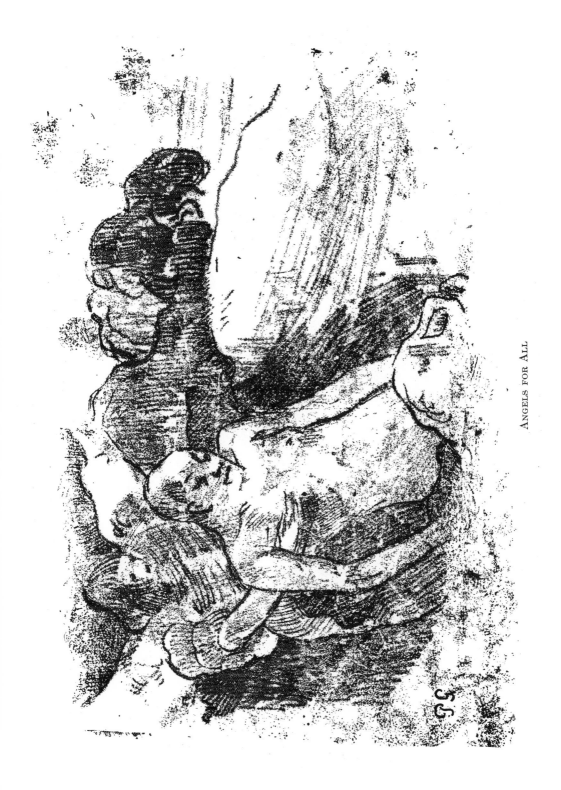

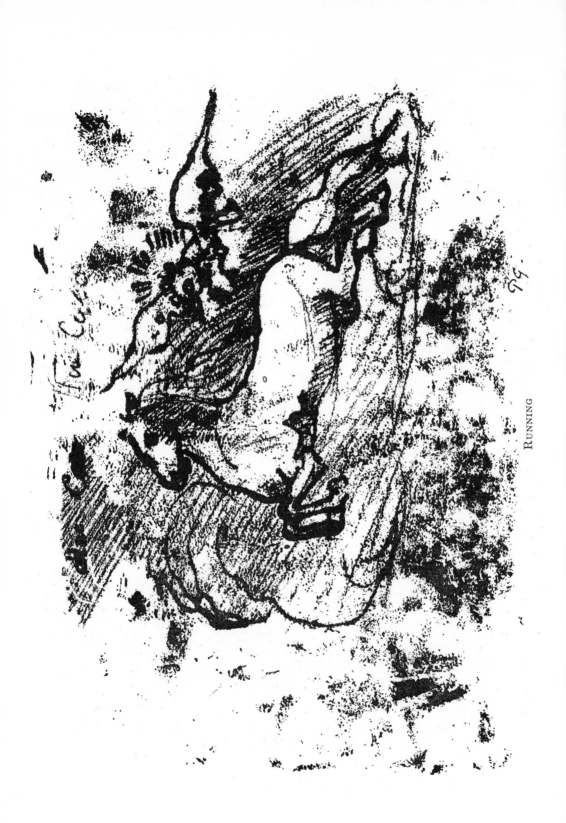

RUNNING

In Ibsen's play, "An Enemy of the People" the wife (at the end only) attains her husband's stature. As commonplace and selfish as the crowd, if not more so—during her whole life, she has just one moment that melts all the Northern ice in her. And she goes to the land where the wolves live.

That may have been carefully studied from nature, though I doubt it, being myself humanly concerned in a way. It takes very little to bring about a woman's fall, but you have to lift a whole world in order to lift her.

I know another enemy of the people whose wife not only did not follow her husband, but has even brought up the children so well that they do not know their father,—so well that this father, who is still in the country of the wolves, has never heard "dear Father" murmured in his ear. At his death, if there is anything to inherit, they will turn up.

Enough—

However it may be about this conclusion, the play suddenly goes to pieces. A literary work, a play for the theatre, is not a work of chance; subject as it is to the necessities of convention and observation, its margin of sentiment must be carefully measured in the light of verisimilitude.

In Zola's *Pot-Bouille* Madame Josserand remains throughout the same Madame Josserand.

On this subject I am far from competent; but without in any way contesting Ibsen's genius, I should like to say that we French are just as serious, perhaps, without being so heavy. In this mythology of the North the winds seem to me very rough and they send me out in search of a ray of sunlight.

All these pastors, these professors, these young girls who, however sentimental they may be, never forget to eat good, hearty meals, smoked fish and ham, not to forget the game,—all these people appear on our French stage like heavy statues. They are solidly built, it is true, but a Greek sculptor would have wanted to refine them.

In the hands of a Rodin I should begin to like them. Ibsen studies them with his eye. It is a good thing for us to study them too, for fear of a Protestant invasion, an invasion of these practical-spirited betrothals in which one plays with Everything-but-not-that, and this muddy philosophy that rides roughshod over the proprieties.

In the scales of the North, the largest heart cannot resist a hundred-sou piece. I too have observed the North, and the best thing I found there was assuredly not my mother-in-law, but the game she cooked so admirably. The fish is excellent, too. Before marriage, everything is warm and friendly, but afterwards, look out, it all goes to pieces.

In Copenhagen, a great lady forgets her purse, which is marked with her monogram, and leaves it behind her in a shop. In her purse there is a condom. But in an attic in my house a couple were living together unmarried. They were promptly marched off to gaol.

Apropos of Ibsen, and speaking of the theatre, it seems to me that here we have a prospective corpse, something we cannot save, but that we might like to stuff, in order to show it to the crowd—at a distance, to make them believe it still exists.

Certainly the literary art of the theatre demands the right to live; that I freely grant. Thank God, there are still readers. But with nothing but readers, I believe the art of the theatre, removed from the theatre, would gain. In the theatre itself, there are scenic exigencies that cramp the author; and from the very first, the production constrains the actors and the public.

On the stage, only three things exist, the actors, the problem or entertainment, and the scenery. It is all theatricality and sham.

When a mother has lost her child and finds it again, it is not the preceding words that bring tears to the eye, even the cry, "Heaven be praised! my daughter!" but the actual appearance of the dear little creature saying "Mamma!"

A Sardou and a few good actors are all you need in the theatre. Do not scold Sardou; he is the only one who has the right idea. By all sorts of tricks and dodges they try to prove the contrary. "The education of the public . . . an enlightened public," etc. . . .

Say an enlightened reading public and you will be right.

On the stage, the bourgeois in Labiche's plays is an atrocious clown; when you read the play the bourgeois is a very good sort, a man you respect. You get from it all a certain sort of domestic philosophy that is thoroughly good and likable.

"But," you will say, "on the stage the actor strengthens the emotion and clarifies the situation." Does an enlightened public need that?

And if the author is really great, why call in others? For in that case, who is to tell us that, however enlightened we may be, our emotion does not spring entirely from the actors and the scenery?

The plain fact, confess it, is that the theatre makes money. Well, then, go ahead as Sardou does, he is clever enough to have the knack of the theatre.

Does the spoken word really belong to literature? If it does, how tiresome it is in its unreality and its pedantry! Put on that play of Remy de Gourmont's[1] and see if the old king, the father, is not a deplorable simpleton, the daughters atrocious ghouls, and all the combatants knights of the Mardi Gras. But when it is read, it is quite another thing.

The director of the Théâtre de l'Œuvre says to us, quite reasonably: "Give me good plays, but plays that can be acted."

Paul Fort, who founded this theatre, was far too much of an artist not to foresee the approaching death of the literary theatre and has given up his project in order to write admirable plays that cannot be acted.

I could collect the greatest number of examples without convincing a single soul; this I know. But as a lover, in my way, of the literary art, I am saying what I think here.

My own theatre is Life; in it I find everything, actors and scenery, the noble and the trivial, tears and laughter.

Often, when I am moved, I cease to be the auditor and become the actor. One could not believe how, in the primitive life, one's opinions change or how the theatre widens. Nothing troubles my judgment, not even the judgment of others. I look at the stage whenever I, and I alone, choose, without any constraint, without even a pair of gloves.

*

*　　　*

I have written somewhere, and my opinion has not changed, that reading in Paris was not the same thing as reading in the woods.

In Paris, one is in a hurry. In a restaurant, eating, I could never read anything but the newspaper. In the post office, I read my letters on the spot, even though I read them over again later. On a railway train, I invariably read "The Three Musketeers." At home I read the dictionary. On the other hand, I never read books of which I had already read criticisms. So far as I am concerned, advertising is thrown away. The most I might do, from having seen the posters, would be to taste Bornibus Mustard. Here I am lying to you atrociously, for I do not like mustard. But forewarned is forearmed!

Do not attempt to read Edgar Poe except in some very reassuring spot. Brave as you may be, without ever having shown it (as Verlaine says), you

[1] I do not remember the title; the play was published in the *Mercure*.

will smart for it. And especially do not try to go to sleep afterwards in sight of an Odilon Redon.

Let me tell you a true story.

My wife and I were both of us reading by the fire. Outside it was cold. My wife was reading "The Black Cat" by Edgar Poe and I "Bonheur dans le Crime" by Barbey d'Aurevilly.

The fire was going out and it was cold outside. Someone had to go after coal. My wife went down into the cellar of the little house which we had rented from the painter Jobbé-Duval.

On the steps, a black cat gave a frightened jump; so did my wife. But after a little hesitation she continued on her way. She had taken two shovelfuls when a skull rolled out from the coal. Transfixed with terror, my wife dropped everything in the cellar, dashed back up the stairway and then fainted in the room. I went down in my turn, and as I set about getting the coal I brought to light a whole skeleton.

It was an old jointed skeleton which had been used by the painter Jobbé-Duval, who had flung it down cellar when it had fallen to pieces.

As you see, it was all extremely simple; and yet the coincidence was strange. Beware of Edgar Poe! Returning to my reading and remembering the black cat, I could not help thinking of the panther which serves as a prelude to that extraordinary story, Barbey d'Aurevilly's "Bonheur dans le Crime."

Often, too, in reading, one comes across an incident related by the author exactly like one that has happened to oneself.

I used to go sometimes on Tuesdays to the house of that admirable man and poet, Stéphane Mallarmé. On one of these Tuesdays they were talking about the Commune, and I talked about it also.

Returning from the Bourse some time after the events of the Commune, I had gone into the Café Mazarin. At a table I saw a gentleman with a military air, who strongly resembled an old schoolmate, and as I looked at him a little too attentively, he said to me haughtily, pulling his moustache, "Do I owe you something?"

"Excuse me," I answered, "were you not at Lorial? My name is Paul Gauguin."

Said he, "My name is Dennebonde."

We at once remembered one another and began to tell each other what had happened to us. He was an officer who had graduated from St. Cyr, had been taken prisoner by the Prussians and had commanded a battalion at the entrance of the troops from Versailles into Paris. Arriving with his battalion by way of the Champs Elysées at the Place de la Concorde, and then going up to the Gare St. Lazare, he encountered a barricade made by the prisoners. Among these prisoners was a brave little Paris gamin of about thirteen, who had been caught with a gun in his hand.

"Excuse me, captain," said the youngster; "before I die I should like to go and say goodbye to my poor grandmother who lives up in the attic you see there; but don't be uneasy, I shan't be long."

"Be off with you then!"

I wanted to wring the hand of this good Dennebonde, the comrade of my childhood; however, I refrained and he continued:

"We went on up the street as far as the Barrière Clichy, but before we had got there, the boy arrived, out of breath, exclaiming, 'Here I am, captain!'"

And I, Gauguin, curious, asked, "What did you do?"

"Well," he said, "I shot him. You understand, my duty as a soldier . . ."

From that moment I have believed that I understood what this famous "soldier's conscience" is. As the waiter was passing, I paid for the drinks without a word and took myself off, presto, instanter, thoroughly upset.

Stéphane Mallarmé went to look for a superb volume of Victor Hugo, and in that magician's voice of his which he managed so well, he began to read aloud the little tale I have just told you, only at the end Hugo, too respectful of humanity, did not have the young hero shot.

I was embarrassed, afraid they might think I had been taking them in. Happily, the right sort of people understand one another, do they not?

The mere cover of a book bearing the name of Lamartine brings to my mind my adorable mother who never lost an opportunity to read her *Jocelyn*.

Books! What memories!

The Marquis de Sade, I assure you, has no interest for me, but it is not on account of virtue, heaven knows!

*
*   *

Before me is the photograph of a painting by Degas.

The lines of the floor run toward a very high and far-away point on the horizon; a line of dancers crosses them in a rhythmical progress, full of manner, ordained in advance. Their studied gaze is directed toward the male in the foreground, in the corner at the left. Harlequin, one hand on his hip, the other holding a mask. He is gazing too. What is the symbol? Is it eternal love, the traditional antics that are called coquetry? Not at all. It is choreography.

Below, a portrait of Holbein's from the Dresden Gallery. Very small hands, too small, without bones or muscles. These hands annoy me. "These hands," I say, "are not Holbein's."

One thing leads to another, which makes me speak of something else that annoys me, the appraising of pictures by men who cannot possibly be experts. All the picture-sales are conducted by men who are at the same time auctioneers, experts and dealers. Now, it is the same with dealers as with critics (especially dealers)—they talk about things of which they know nothing. Although the dealer sometimes has an intuition about the rise and fall of prices, still he sees only the moment; he always approaches the future with his finger in his eye. When the question is one of the authenticity or the spuriousness of a picture, he knows nothing. Does he know whether the picture is good or bad? Never! It is a great misfortune for the painter not to have a dealer who is capable of recognizing his talent.

Once this is admitted—and it must be admitted, it is so obvious—what are we to say of this title "Expert"!!? Experts who force themselves upon you, and whom you have to pay through the nose!

*

*   *

In regard to the allegory, the symbol, the emblems in the public monuments of our good city of Paris, they flounder about a good deal.

The writer can never be represented without his old book and his goose-quill. The inventor of a syringe must have his clyster-pipe.

If they ever raise a statue to H. G. Wells in London, I shall demand that he has his Heat-Ray. But if they put up a statue some day to Santos-Dumont, will they have to sculpture a balloon? And how, in the case of Pasteur, will they indicate the culture of microbes?

Another thing that appears of no importance and yet is important is the glorification of Agriculture, Pisciculture, etc., in allegories that are fifty feet above ground. At the Trocadero, the whole roof is decorated in this way without our being able to say whether the decorations are masterpieces or turnips. And where is the signature? If the intention is to patronize the arts, the artists should be recompensed. Admitting this, let us bring it all down and ornament the lower galleries. But there you are! Among these artists there are some whose reputation would fall even lower.

There are people who call themselves Spaniards who are nothing but sham Spaniards.

At the Hôtel de Ville, the same thing is true. From their niches, the provosts of Paris look down upon us from above and find us very small. We look up at them also, to see if the day is fair, and find them even smaller.

Sometimes, looking up in the air, one sees strange things. A young Danish girl who was dancing in our capital was walking along one day near Notre Dame. Hearing some crows cawing she raised her head and saw a curious black flag, shaped like a flame, detach itself from one of the towers. This flag zigzagged in a strange way. It was a young woman who was hanging from the iron railing, where the stanchion had pierced her breast. (*Souvenirs de la Morgue.*)

A competition is going on for a public monument: there is a sculptor, and an architect for the pedestal. The sculptor considers that a large pedestal will spoil his statue; the architect considers that his pedestal ought to be the important thing.

In this monument, which is the roast and which is the gravy?

Oh, these competitions!

Fortunately Saint Peter's at Rome was not decorated by the competition-method.

In the competition for the famous chariot that was to adorn the Arc de Triomphe, I saw Falguière's rough model. It was, as they say, capitally hit off. There was a suppleness in the horse's flanks that enchanted us.

Once the monument was in place, I could see nothing but the bellies of the horses. A well-known sculptor to whom I made this observation replied, "After all, a figure placed high up ought to look as the living subject would if it were placed in the same position." Hum! Hum!

I was dining one day with Dalou at the house of this well-known sculptor, and he said to me, "Monsieur, sculpture will be republican or it will cease to exist."

Outdone, Déroulède!

Young men who go in for art will not find the nourishing milk they need in a tin. Here the School is the tin.

Be stingy of nothing but the name of friend, and take care not to waste your insults.

People are always borrowing from Dégas but he does not complain. His purse of malice is so full that a pebble more or less does not impoverish him.

Albert Wolff in the *Figaro:*
"Posterity always establishes men in their proper rank, pulling down from their pedestals those who have been lifted up through deceit, in order to make place for others who have the right to it. For this reason the great ones who are unknown may continue on their way in the conviction of eternal justice, which is often tardy but always certain at the time appointed."
Albert Wolff? A crocodile.

                              *
              *   *

My grandmother was an amusing old lady. Her name was Flora Tristan. Proudhon said she had genius. Knowing nothing about this, I take Proudhon's word for it.

She was connected with all sorts of socialist affairs, among them the workers' unions. The grateful workers set up a monument to her in the cemetery of Bordeaux. It is probable that she did not know how to cook. A socialist-anarchist blue-stocking! To her, in association with Père Enfantin, was attributed the founding of a certain religion, the religion of Mapa, in which Enfantin was the god Ma and she the goddess Pa.

Between the truth and the fable I have never been able to distinguish, and I offer you this for what it is worth. She died in 1844; many delegations followed her coffin. What I can tell you with confidence, however, is that Flora Tristan was a very pretty and noble lady. She was an intimate friend of Madame Desbordes-Valmore. I also know that she spent her whole fortune in the workers' cause, travelling ceaselessly. Between whiles she went to Peru to see her uncle, Citizen Don Pio de Tristan de Moscoso (of an Aragonese family).

Her daughter, who was my mother, was brought up entirely in a school, the Pension Bascans, an establishment that was essentially republican. It was there that my father, Clovis Gauguin, made her acquaintance. My father was at that time the political correspondent of the *National*, the journal of Thiers and Armand Marast.

Did my father, after the events of '48 (I was born 7 June, '48), foresee the *coup d'etat* of 1852? I do not know. However that may be, he took it

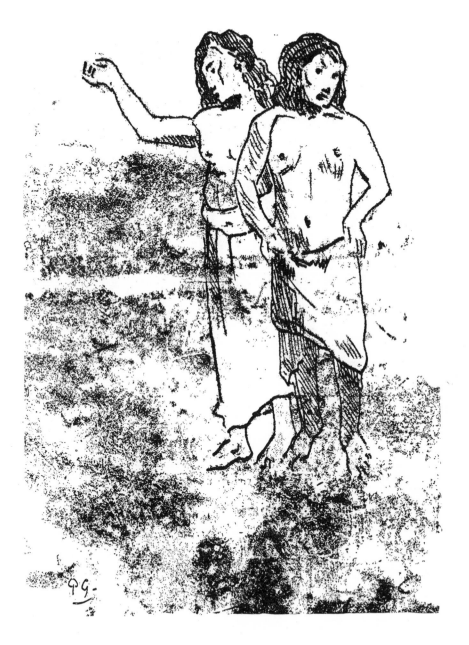

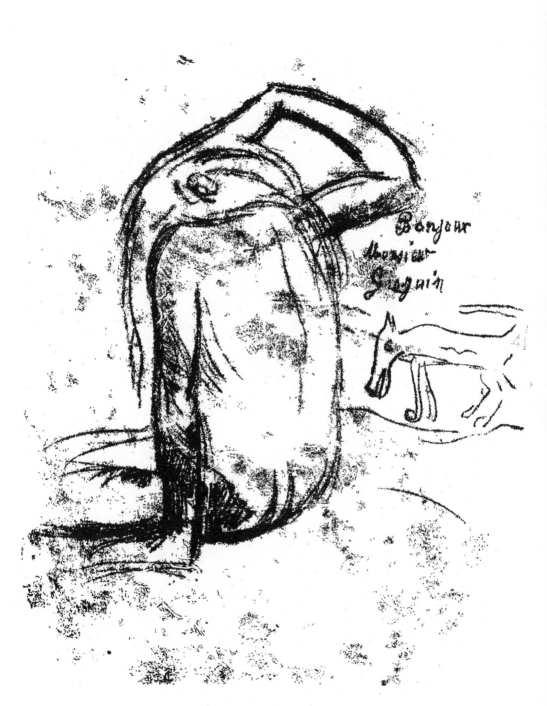

Bonjour
Monsieur
Gauguin

Ta Orana

into his head to set out for Lima, intending to start a newspaper there. The young household possessed a certain fortune.

He had the bad luck to fall in with a certain captain, a terrible person who did him an atrocious injury when he already had a serious case of heart-trouble. Just as he was starting to land at Port Famine, in the Straits of Magellan, he collapsed in the jolly-boat and died of a ruptured blood-vessel.

This is not a book, nor is it my memoirs, and if I talk to you about my life, it is because at the moment my mind is full of memories of my childhood.

My old, old uncle, Don Pio, quite lost his heart to his niece, who was so pretty and so much like his dearly-loved brother, Don Mariano. Don Pio had remarried at the age of eighty and had several children from this new marriage, among others Etchenique, who for years was President of Peru.

All these constituted a numerous family, and among them my mother was a veritable spoiled child.

I have a remarkable visual memory and I recall this time of my life, our house and ever so many things that happened; the monument at the Presidency, the church the dome of which was entirely of carved wood, put on later. I still see the little negro girl who, as the custom was, carried to church the little rug on which we knelt to pray. I also see that Chinese servant of ours who was so clever at ironing. He was the one who found me in a grocery-shop, sitting between two barrels of molasses, busily sucking sugar-cane, while my weeping mother was having them search for me everywhere. I have always had a fancy for running away in this fashion; at Orleans, when I was nine years old, I took it into my head to run away to the forest of Bondy with a handkerchief full of sand at the end of a stick which I carried over my shoulder.

It was a picture that had beguiled me, a picture representing a traveller with his stick and bundle over his shoulder. Beware of pictures! Fortunately, the butcher took me by the hand on the road and, calling me a rascal, led me back to my mother's.

As was natural in a very noble Spanish lady, my mother was quick-tempered, and I received some slaps from her little hand, which was as flexible as rubber. It is true that a few minutes later my mother kissed and caressed me, weeping.

But not to anticipate, let us return to our city of Lima. In those days in Lima, that delicious country where it never rained, the roofs were terraces. If there was a lunatic in the household he had to be kept at home; these lunatics would be kept on the terrace, fastened by a chain to a ring, and the owner of the house or the tenant was obliged to provide them with a certain amount of very simple food. I remember that once my sister, the little negress and I, who were sleeping in a room the open door of which gave on to an inner court, were awakened and saw opposite us a madman climbing down the ladder. The moon lighted up the court. Not one of us dared to utter a word. I saw, I can still see, the madman enter our room, glance at us, and then quietly climb up again to his terrace.

Another time I was awakened at night and saw the superb portrait of my uncle, which hung in the room, with its eyes fixed on us, *moving*.

It was an earthquake.

Brave as you may be, wise even as you may be, you tremble when the earth trembles. That is a sensation common to everybody and which no one would ever deny.

I realized this later, at a time when I was in the roads at Iquique and saw part of the town crumble and the waves play with the ships as if they were balls tossed by a racquet. I have never wanted to be a Freemason, unwilling as I am, either from an instinct of liberty or a lack of sociability, to belong to any society. But I recognize the value of this institution among sailors. In these same roads of Iquique I saw a trading brig dragged loose by a very powerful tide-wave and driven to destruction on the rocks. It hoisted to the top of the mast its Freemason's pennant, and at once most of the ships in the harbour sent it their small boats to tow it off with bowlines. As a result it was saved.

My mother loved to tell about her pranks at the Presidency. Among them was this.

A high officer in the army, who had Indian blood in his veins, had boasted of being very fond of pimento. At a dinner to which this officer had been invited, my mother ordered the cook to prepare two dishes of sweet pimentos. One was prepared as usual, the other was seasoned with a vengeance, with the strongest pimentos. At dinner my mother had herself placed beside him, and while everyone else was served from the ordinary dish, our officer was served from the special dish. He saw nothing but fire when, after having served himself to an enormous helping, he felt the blood rising to his face.

In a very serious voice, my mother asked him, "Is the dish badly seasoned? Don't you find it strong enough?"

"On the contrary, Madame, the dish is excellent." And the unhappy man had the courage to empty his plate to the last mouthful.

How graceful and pretty my mother was when she put on her Lima costume, the silk mantilla covering her face and allowing a glimpse of only one eye, an eye so soft and so imperious, so pure and caressing.

I still see our street with the chickens pecking among the refuse. In those days Lima was not what it is today, a great sumptuous city.

Thus four years passed when, one fine day, urgent letters arrived from France. We had to return to settle an inheritance from my paternal grandfather. My mother, who was so unpractical in business matters, returned to Orleans in France. It was a mistake, for in the following year, 1856, the old uncle, weary of successfully teasing Madame Death for so long, allowed her to get the better of him.

Don Pio de Tristan de Moscoso was no more. He was 113 years old.

In memory of his dearly-loved brother, he had left my mother a yearly income of 5,000 piastres, which came to a little more than 25,000 francs. But the family, at his death-bed, overrode the desires of the old man and took possession of the whole of his immense fortune, which was squandered in Paris in foolish extravagances. One single cousin remained in Lima and lives there still, very rich, a perfect mummy. The mummies of Peru are famous.

The following year, Etchenique came to suggest an arrangement with my mother who, proud as ever, replied that it was "nothing."

Although never in actual poverty, from this time on our life was extremely simple.

Much later, in the year 1880, I think, Etchenique came to Paris again as Ambassador, on a mission to arrange with the Comptoir d'Escompte the guaranty of the Peruvian loan (on a basis of guano).

He stayed with his sister, who had a splendid house in the rue de Chaillot, and, being a discreet ambassador, gave her to understand that everything was going well. My cousin, pleased by this as all the Peruvians were, hastened to speculate on a rise in the Peruvian loan in the Maison Dreyfus.

But the contrary was true; and a few days later the Peruvian stock was unsalable. She drank up several millions in that soup!

"*Caro mio,*" she said to me, "I am ruined. I have nothing left but the eight horses in the stable. What is to become of me?"

She had two extremely beautiful daughters. I remember one of them, a child of about my own age, whom it appears I tried to violate; at the time I was six years old. The violation could not have done much harm, and we probably both of us thought it was nothing but an innocent game.

As you see, my life has been full of ups and downs and agitations. In myself are many strange mixtures. A rough sailor—so be it! But there is race there also, or rather two races.

I could exist without writing this; but then, why should I not write it?—since I have no other aim than to amuse myself.

*

*   *

And I must needs amuse myself, these days, shut up as I am by the flood on my little island, as I have told you further back. The flood and the storm are hardly over yet; everyone is extricating himself as well as he can, cutting away the uprooted trees and setting up on all sides little foot-bridges, so that one can move from neighbour to neighbour. We are wait-ing for the mail, which does not come; and, realizing that there is little chance of it, we hope that within a year the Administration will repair our disasters and send us a little money.

The post should also bring us a judge to undertake the investigation of a crime. Here is a letter which I have prepared for the judge, a letter that will enlighten you as to the manner in which they administer the French colonies.

To the Police Magistrate

Atuana, January, 1903.

Permit me to inform you of certain facts in connection with this murder which you are going to investigate. They concern a man who, for lack of evidence on his behalf, may perhaps be falsely condemned for murder.

We, the public, are imperfectly informed about what the police-sergeant has said in his declaration; on the other hand, we know all that has *not* been done, because we have taken the trouble to do the work ourselves.

But is it our business to do police work?

The sergeant must have questioned the negro, then, very briefly, the victim and her friend. That was all, and that was practically nothing.

When this had been done, the victim was turned over to be examined and cared for by a hospital orderly who, although he has undergone a brief apprenticeship in the hospi-tal at Papeete, is still an empty-headed and inexperienced young man.

Two days later, a wide-spread rumour apprised me that this woman had a horrible wound in the vagina that was in an advanced state of decomposition.

Not imagining for a moment that this wound could have passed unobserved, I paid no attention to the matter, and it was not till fifteen days after the affair that the drug-gist came to ask my advice, declaring that, unable to endure her suffering, the woman had admitted that she had a serious wound in the vagina. Gangrene had already set in and death followed.

From this one can be assured that this last wound was the sole cause of the woman's death.

Is the negro the author of it?

And what has been done to find out?

On whom falls the responsibility for this negligence? Certainly not on you, Monsieur, who, arriving here long afterward, are not in a position to be informed.

The police, from the beginning, have contented themselves with a more or less haphazard interrogation of the negro, the victim and the friend.

Since then there has been no inquiry, as if, in spite of everything, they knew or wished to know nothing about this last wound or about the lover, while the public has grown so disturbed that a colonist informed the police-sergeant that, although the lover lived a long way from the negro, he was at the spot at three in the afternoon, in company with the victim and her friend.

That there is a conspiracy to save this lover appears almost obvious.

The police-sergeant knew well enough, as everyone knows here, that Pastor Vernier and I (especially M. Vernier) have quite an extensive knowledge of medicine. Why did he not consult us on this occasion? Out of vanity, no doubt, the stupid, autocratic vanity of a gendarme.

I can declare without hesitation that if I had been called, this third wound would not have passed unobserved, and that it would have been easy for me to tell whether it had been made with a knife.

I do know, however, that the two other wounds were examined and probed, an examination which proved that they had both been made by a knife of medium size and not by a sickle.

This knife should have been found in the brush. If, again, there is a contradiction between the declarations of the two women and the observed fact, are there not grounds for suspecting an interested lie, told to throw justice off the track?

But what is beyond doubt is the complete silence, both before and after, on the subject of this third wound, which caused the death; the unwillingness to accuse anyone, even the negro.

Her lover was at her bedside constantly, urging her with protestations of love intermingled with threats to a silence which the poor victim kept to her last hour.

One is forced inescapably to recognize that there is in all this a great passional interest (a love interest) to save a murderer, the lover himself. What gives even more force to this supposition is that the horrible wound, made so brutally in the vagina, was made with a piece of wood, which tore it everywhere, and of which several slivers (according to the confession of the victim) were drawn by her out of the wound.

That is the work of a native. A number of previous cases have enlightened us about the Marquesan habits and customs. The savage reappears when passion is aroused and he is possessed by the demon of jealousy. He flings himself upon this part of the body, imagining a cruel and murderous coition.

Public rumour as well as logic indicate that it was there they ought to have looked for light upon the mystery. And this was exactly what was not done.

The lover has never been examined or troubled by the police and no one has been questioned about him. I say the police intentionally, for the new sergeant, following the mistakes of his predecessors, wishes to know nothing, nothing at all.

Today, when it is too late, this native could find as many false witnesses as he wished to establish an alibi for him. That is the way in the Marquesas.

Where is our security in the future if the police, always protected by their chiefs, are to continue this sinister tradition, pestering the colonist and the native without ever protecting them? I say this sinister tradition advisedly, for with this method of procedure every crime committed in the Marquesas has always been considered obscure by the court and consequently has always gone unpunished; while the public, which is always informed indirectly, learns the truth at once.

When a crime is committed, the guilty man threatens any indiscreet persons with death, and that is enough. Everyone, if not among his friends, at least officially, holds his tongue, in this way making common cause with the gendarmes, who are so wilfully short-sighted.

PAUL GAUGUIN.

*

*   *

Permit me to present to you a class of individuals of whose existence you have no suspicion. These are the colonial inspectors. Each one of them costs us, on an average, 80,000 francs a year.

They arrive in the colony, as charming as possible, with orders to listen to everyone who has anything to say and distributing false promises everywhere.

When they leave everyone exclaims, "At last!! Now things are going to change. The minister is to hear what is going on."

Turlututu, mon chapeau pointu!

Sometimes, indeed, there are a few changes, but they are always for the worse, and the colonist says, "They'll never catch me again." Which does not prevent him from being caught again, notwithstanding.

I am asking to be caught again, too.

Two inspectors have just reached us in the Marquesas, announced as liberal, charming, intelligent, white blackbirds, in short.

I write to them:

TO THE COLONIAL PASSING THROUGH THE MARQUESAS.

Gentlemen,

You have asked, even urged us to inform you in writing of all that we know concerning the colony and of such reforms as we may desire, all this with whatever comments happen to occur to us.

So far as concerns me personally, I have no wish to lay before you the eternal schema of the financial, administrative and agricultural situation. These are grave questions which have been long debated already and which have this peculiarity, that the more one agitates them, the more complaints one makes, the more one indulges even in violent polemics, the more it all tends to an aggravation of the ills that have been pointed out and to the final ruin of the colony, and the more quickly the maltreated colonist finds himself obliged to set out in search of another and a better land, less despotic and more favourable to life.

I wish merely to beg you to investigate for yourselves the character of the natives here in our Marquesan colony, and the behaviour of the gendarmes toward them; and for this reason.

It is because, for reasons of economy, a judge is sent to us only about once in eighteen months.

Then the judge arrives, in a hurry to pass sentence, knowing nothing, nothing of what the natives are like. Seeing before him a tattooed face, he says to himself, "There's a cannibal brigand," especially when the gendarme, who has an interest in the matter, tells him so. And this is why he tells him so. The gendarme institutes proceedings against thirty persons or so who have been enjoying themselves dancing and a few of whom have been drinking orange-juice. The thirty are sentenced to a fine of 100 francs (here 100 francs are equal to 500 in any other country), which makes 3,000 francs, plus the costs, which also makes 1,000 francs for this gendarme, his third of the fine.

This third of the fine has been suppressed quite recently, but what difference does that make? The tradition is there, and the base desire for vengeance also,—if only to prove that they do their duty in spite of this suppression.

I wish also to point out that *this sum of 3,000 francs alone*, with the costs, exceeds all that the valley can yield in a year. (It is all the worse when there are still other infractions; and that is always the case.)

I wish to point out again that this sentence comes after the disaster of the cyclone that has destroyed all the shoots of the *maiore* (the breadfruit tree), which means that *for six months they will be deprived of their only food.*

Is this human, is this ethical?

The judge arrives, then, and by his own will establishes himself at the gendarmerie, takes his meals there and sees no one but the police-sergeant, who gives him the records along with his own opinions. "This one . . . that one . . . all brigands. You see, your honour, if we were not severe with these people, we should all be murdered. . . ." And the judge is convinced.

Whether or not there is any understanding between them, I do not know.

At the hearing, the accused is questioned through the mediation of an interpreter who knows none of the fine shades of the language and who especially does not know the language of the court, a language very difficult to interpret in this primitive tongue, except by the use of much paraphrase.

Thus, for example, they ask an accused native if he has been drinking. He answers, "No," and the interpreter says, "He says he has never drunk." And the judge exclaims, "But he has already been convicted for drunkenness!"

The native, by nature very timid in the presence of the European, who seems to him very learned and his superior, remembering also the *guns* of former days, appears before the Tribunal terrified by the gendarmes, the presiding judge, etc., and prefers to confess even when he is innocent, knowing that a denial will entail a still severer punishment. The reign of terror!

I may say that there is a gendarme who has instituted proceedings against several natives who have not wished to send their children to the bishop's school, a parochial school inscribed in the year-book as a *Free School!*

I may say also that the judge has convicted them!!

Is this legal?

In regard to these natives, there are gendarmes in certain posts who have absolute power, whose word is law with the court, which has no immediate control, and whose one concern is to line their own pockets, living on the backs of the natives, who are generous, poor as they are. The gendarme frowns, and the native hands over chickens, eggs, pigs, etc. Otherwise, beware of infractions!

When, by some chance—it is not easy—a colonist with a little courage catches a gendarme in some delinquency, immediately everybody falls on this colonist. And the worst that can happen to the gendarme is a little so-called admonition from his lieutenant (behind closed doors) and a change of post. The gendarme here is rough, ignorant, venal and ferocious in the performance of his duties, but very skillful in covering his tracks. Thus, if he receives a jug of wine, you may be sure that he has a receipted bill in his pocket. But how is one to prove officially what everyone knows outside of court?

And I am not considering that, besides holding his post as gendarme, he is a notary here, a special under-agent, a tax-collector, a sheriff's officer, a harbour-master, everything, in short, but a man warranted to be honest and intelligent.

It is to be noted, however, that he is always married, not to count the numerous mistresses who always yield for fear of court proceedings against them because they have been seen in the river without the regulation vine-leaf.

71

It is to be noted, besides, that, however humble his wife's condition may be, she can never get along without a servant, and that for this he takes anyone he can lay his hands on, even a prisoner or the prison guard—and all at the expense of the tax-payers.

But if there is a crime, a murder . . . everything is changed. The gendarme, afraid for his own safety, hastens to encourage silence, goes to the left when he ought to go to the right and questions no one, not even the colonists, saying that when the magistrate comes he will see about it all. (Consult the record of crimes, and especially the last one, a case tried at Atuana in February, 1903.)

Aside from the crimes, which are fortunately very rare, as the population in general is very mild, there remain nothing but such misdemeanours as drunkenness.

As the natives have nothing, nothing at all to amuse them, they are always, on all occasions, having recourse to the drinks which nature has furnished them gratis, made from orange-juice, the flowers of the cocoanut, bananas, etc., fermented for a few days and less harmful than our alcoholic drinks in Europe.

Since this quite recent prohibition, which has suppressed a trade that is remunerative for the colonists, the native thinks of one thing only, drinking, and for this he leaves the villages in order to hide elsewhere. To this is due the impossibility of finding labourers. We might as well tell them to return to savagery.

What is worse, the mortality is increasing.

The gendarme attends to his business, which is man-hunting.

A lofty morality, as you see.

I therefore ask the Inspectors to investigate the question seriously in order to request of the authorities in France, those men who concern themselves with justice and humanity, what I am going to request of them:

1. In order that the courts in the Marquesas may be respectworthy and respected, I ask that the judges should rigorously avoid any but business relations with the gendarmerie, lodging and taking their meals elsewhere. They are paid for this.

2. That the judge should not accept the gendarme's reports except after they have been carefully verified and official information has been sought even among the colonists, a proceeding he would find very useful to him; and above all, that he should not invoke the law except where the gendarme has acted *according to regulations*. And *to this end* I ask that the rules governing the gendarmerie should be posted in the office of this gendarmerie so that any infraction of these rules, committed by a gendarme, should come at once before the Court of Appeals and be severely punished.

3. I ask that the fines for drinking should be proportioned to the wealth of the country, for it is immoral and inhuman that a country which yields only 50,000 francs from its products should have fines of more than 75,000 francs imposed on it. The taxes, the payments in kind and the duties which, by the way, go into another coffer than that of the colony, are at the absolute disposition of the governor.

This is the situation, gentlemen; verify the figures while you are here.

I ask also that the gendarmes' reports shall not be accepted without question by the court till the time comes when they can be carefully verified, as they are in our country, till the native population is capable (knowing the French language) of bearing witness against the gendarme without being terrorized, and also without passing through the hands of an interpreter, who is inclined to be over-cautious, completely dependent as he is on the good will of the police (his position depends on it) and who, moreover, as can easily be proved, knows French *very imperfectly*.

If, on the one hand, you make special laws to prevent them from drinking, although Europeans and negroes are allowed to do so, while, on the other hand, their statements, their affirmations before the court count for nothing, it is preposterous to tell them that they are French electors, and to impose on them schools and other religious nonsense.

There is a singular irony in this hypocritical esteem for Liberty, Equality, Fraternity under a French flag, when one thinks of this revolting spectacle of men who are no longer anything but so much flesh, taxed in every way and at the mercy of the gendarme. And with all this they are obliged to cry, Hurrah for the Governor! Hurrah for the Republic!

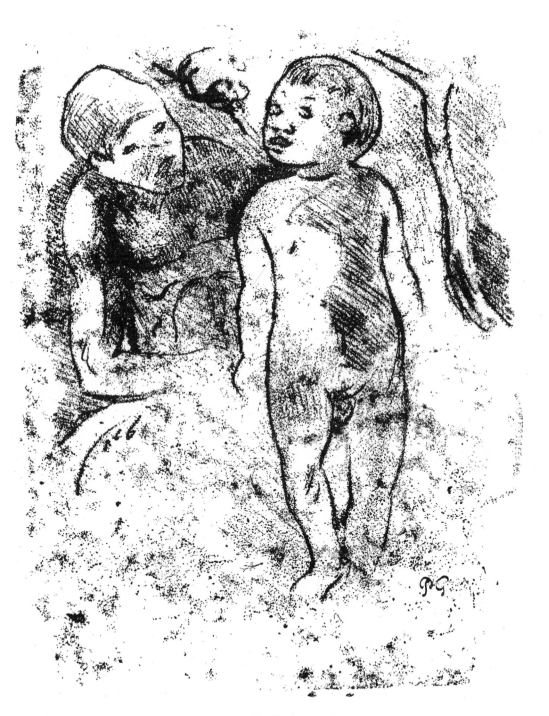

TE TAMARI

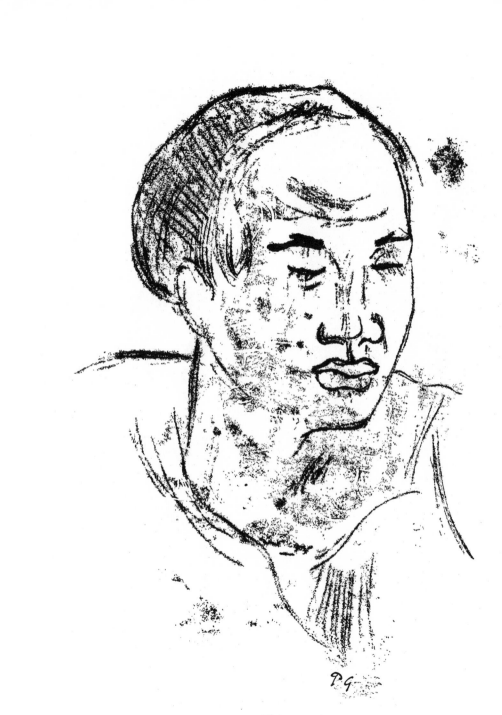

STUDY

When July 14 arrives, they find in their cash-box only 400 francs for their own expenses, while, in addition to their direct and indirect taxes, they have paid more than 30,000 in fines.

We colonists believe, therefore, that this is a dishonour to the French Republic, and you must not be surprised if some foreigner here says to you, "I am very glad I am not a Frenchman," while the Frenchman says to you, "I wish the Marquesas belonged to America."

To sum up, what are we asking? That justice shall be justice, and not empty words, and that, to bring this about, they send us competent men, men of kindly feelings who will study the question on the spot and afterwards act energetically . . . in the open.

When, by chance, the governors pass through here, it is only to take photographs. A responsible person who dares to speak to them and ask them to rectify an injustice gets nothing but rudeness and punishment for his pains.

There, gentlemen, is all I have to tell you. It may be of interest to you—unless you consider with Pangloss that "everything is for the best in the best of possible worlds."

*

*   *

We never really know what stupidity is until we have experimented on ourselves. Sometimes you say to yourself, Good heavens, what an idiot I was! It is just because of this that you perceive you might have done otherwise. Unfortunately, you are already old before you observe that the time has come for reflection. Let us therefore leave things as they are, since we are unable to do otherwise; let us live outside of the schools and consequently without constraint.

Just now, the police-sergeant is very busy telling the natives that he is the boss and not Monsieur Gauguin.

What are they doing in there?

He and Pandora are a pair.

Little Taia, who does his washing, is no fool. When she wants to wheedle ten sous out of him, she says, "You are very wise," and he gives them to her.

"I am the boss here, not Monsieur Gauguin!"

What do you think of little Taia? I offer her to you as a true Marquesan. Big round eyes, a fish's mouth with a row of teeth capable of opening a box of sardines for you. Do not leave it with her long, for she will eat it. In any case, she already knows her sergeant by heart.

This sergeant is the very same one who, once upon a time, in the lower islands, had to bring back a man who had been accidentally drowned, his leg having been bitten off by a shark. He hesitated to put him in the coffin, and the lieutenant impatiently said to him, "What are you waiting for?"

"Excuse me, Lieutenant, but there's a leg missing."

73

"Well, put him in without his leg."

"Excuse me, Lieutenant, but there are some worms . . ."

"Well, put him in, worms and all."

He is the boss, not Monsieur Gauguin.

On his breast the medals shine in all their brilliancy. On his rubicund visage the alcohol shines without brilliancy. In testimony whereof, consequently, subsequently, we have given him his certificate of identity, followed by his description. Salute him, for he is the boss. Forward march! Right wheel! Gee up, old nag! Look out, he kicks, whether he has shoes or not!

*
*   *

Remembering certain theological studies of my youth, and certain later reflections on these subjects, certain discussions also, I took it into my head to establish a sort of parallel between the Gospel and the modern scientific spirit, and upon this the confusion between the Gospel and the dogmatic and absurd interpretation of it in the Catholic church, an interpretation that has made it the victim of hatred and scepticism.

There were a hundred pages, entitled "The Modern Spirit and Catholicism." Indirectly, very indirectly, I got these manuscript sheets into the hands of the bishop.

To crush me, no doubt, he sent me in reply—indirectly also—an enormous book filled with illustrations from photographs and documents of the history of the Church from its beginning.

Still very indirectly, I managed to return with the book my appreciations—criticisms, if you will.

It was the end of the discussion. Here is my reply to this book:

Before us, in our care, to be read by a profane man—a sacred book.

France on the cover. Hum!! *Rome* would be more exact.

"The French Catholic Missions in the Nineteenth Century."

Are they French? That is doubtful. Whatever they may be, France protects and Rome commands. . . . A charming concordat.

430 pages published with great splendour; photographs in confirmation of the text; the collaboration of twelve dignitaries.

Before speaking of the 96 pages of the Introduction, the only contestable part of the book, we wish to express here our profound wonder, our disgust, also, at the notable (and incontestable) labour that one observes in the second part of the book. The edified reader can survey the Orient without the help of the Élisée Reclus Geography.

The College of the Holy Family at Cairo.

Saint Francis Xavier's at Alexandria.

Here are two monuments quite sufficient in themselves to prove that it is not the Church but the French Republic which has taken the vow of poverty.

Notre Dame de Sion at Ramleh and especially the Sisters of Nazareth at Beyrout eclipse any palace.

Let us hope that a new Sardanapalus will not transform these palaces into houses of pleasure and take all these charming nuns as slaves of the flesh.

What better argument can there be against this Church than the display of all this wealth and this almost unequalled power in the hands of a single man, clothed by himself with the mantle of infallibility?

Two thousand years of the Christian era to reach such a result, with the aid of all the sovereigns and torrents of blood and tears poured out for the cupidity of a few who have taken, by force or consent, the gold of the faithful. In the name of Charity!

Is not this significant? Today they no longer say, "We are great." They say, "We are rich."

The political history of the Catholic Church, and especially of the work of the Congregations, the regular army, very carefully documented and admirably described in this book, brings us almost brutally face to face with an infernal machine, with a well-organized and almost imperceptible system of wheels. We knew about it already, but it was a good thing for the Church to state it all precisely and positively for us.

This political history forms the greater part of the Introduction, and it interests us only moderately; it leaves room for only a few lines of theology, if one may call theology a series of arguments to explain the *raison d'être* of this Church. A series of arguments altogether extraordinary and contradictory to an attentive reader who is accustomed to such exercises, but which, twisted from their true sense by this hair-splitting spirit of rhetoric, so peculiar to the disciples of Loyola, have quite a deceptive air of truth.

Let us examine them for a few moments.

Page 4. "Philosophy has Reason for its guide."

Page 8. "The third form of idolatry, the belief in public and national deities, destroys another essential element of civilization, *peace*. Civilization cannot have a lie as its foundation."

Page 10. "But idolatries, powerless to keep societies and individuals in order by moral laws, have had to assure this order through the Artifice of a strong hierarchy which keeps the peoples stable."

An artful and contradictory conclusion.

But let us continue. At another point. Plato said, "To know the Creator and the Father of all things is a difficult undertaking, and when one has known him, it is impossible to explain him to everyone."

Page 12. "Instead of belonging to a caste of nobles, China belongs to a caste of scholars and all rights belong to the intelligence."

Here we must complete the information given. In China, all rights do indeed belong to the intelligence, and all positions are given as the result of competitions between these scholars. But these scholars cannot form a caste any more than the scholars in Europe form a caste today. Everyone has the right of entrance to it.

It is to be noted that Plato, Confucius and the Gospel all agree on this point, that of a society directed by an intellectual aristocracy, animated by the sentiment of justice and based on Reason and Science, instructing the others, the incapable, only in the simplest precepts of honesty, such as the laws of Moses, which the doctors of law must maintain publicly, either by the clearness of their spoken teachings or by the simplicity of a mode of writing which is easily understood.

The Gospel is most explicit on this point, and seems to bear out the conclusion of all the philosophers. It seems to foresee the future with extreme lucidity, and never ceases to warn us against a Church that will not be based on Reason and Science. "Seal up what I say unto you. To you alone belongs the kingdom of heaven; as for the others, it shall be spoken unto them only in parables, in order that. . . ." It urges simplicity, even poverty, contempt for riches.

In contrast with this, if we reflect on what has preceded, we can only conclude that this Church attempts, with a complete denial of these precepts, to invoke them, on the one hand, and on the other to avow the necessity of the *Artifice* of a strong hierarchy in order to keep the peoples stable.

And it adds, "It was when all the philosophies and all the religions had shown themselves powerless to explain life and keep men to their duty, that the Christ appeared. Through Him Faith appears founded upon Reason, and Reason springs from the certitudes of Faith:

"'Love thy neighbour as thyself.

"'Do unto others as ye would that they should do unto you.'"

Excuse me! This is not from the Gospel but from Confucius (the book Tchoung-Youngow). When the author says, "It was then that the Christ appeared," he commits a serious error, for Christolatry, after having been for a long time purely astronomical, became terrestrial at least 3,000 years before the Christian era.

The Christ of the Gospels is, therefore, only the continuation of the ancient Tatu Messiah, with this difference (a difference which the Church hastens to deny) that he became essentially the *son of man*, which is indeed the only comprehensible, reasonable, human basis, since science has killed all supernaturalism, the basis of that superstition which is opposed to civilization.

Superstition which is the *Artifice!*

The Catholic Church, during the first five centuries of the Christian era, not understanding, not wishing to understand its import, strove, in spite of the efforts of a few men, to replace with this Artifice the whole grandeur of the new philosophy. And in this it succeeded. That is what it means.

Page 18. "The struggle that has since taken place to substitute this civilizing morality for the errors of the credulous, the enmity of races and the egoism of the passions has become the greatest fact in history. From the time of Christ to the present day, it has been continued ceaselessly throughout the centuries by the Apostolate."

Page 21. "Christ was the study of all these schools, and most of them saw in him only a man; that was to see in the Church only a human character."

Here is clearly indicated the situation which the Catholic Church has wished to establish, that is to say, to rebuff Reason in everyone, to continue the ancient idolatry, to crush under foot the new humane philosophy which is so well qualified to bring happiness to all in the future, comprising, as it does, all the progress that man, supported by science, can acquire, together with the example of Jesus, the son of man.

Her excuse is the necessity for *Artifice* in order to lead the submissive peoples as she likes—while, in complete contradiction, she takes as the foundation for this Church, "On this rock shall I build my church." This rock, which is Reason itself and not superstition!

And why, too, this strange, fine-spun argument, so apt to deceive everyone: "Through Christ Faith appears, founded upon Reason, and Reason springs from the certitudes of Faith." In French that means absolutely nothing, but its implications are as wide as the world.

This Reason which, as it springs up, becomes reasonable only when it accepts as certitude superstition, artificial superstition,.the only thing that can lead the peoples!

These collaborators are all quite right in submerging these few deceptive pages under the documented political history of this Church, which has become powerful enough to conquer the world, by terror, bloodshed and the help of all the kings.

In all this, where is Reason, where is Faith even, outside of this accumulation of all power and all wealth?

In short, this book displays to us (in addition to their infamous behaviour) a sumptuous edifice of marble and gold, not the edifice of Saint Peter or that of the Gospel.

*

*   *

In the political history of these missions, described in this book, one passage is especially noteworthy because of the timeliness of its bearing today.

Speaking of Confucius, the author says, "As they found in him a portion of the *Christian verities*, they considered that his authority would prove a security for them. The majority of the Jesuits thought it was extreme to forbid, on the pretence of possible danger, practices which might well be innocent and which four hundred million men would not renounce.

"The Jesuits lived at court or in the provinces; they made the most useful conquests among the mandarins. Among this élite the doctrines of Confucius had been preserved most purely.

"Finally, on July 11, 1742, Benedict XIV, with the bull *Exquo singulari*, annulled all these dispensations and once for all condemned the Chinese ceremonies. From that moment the spread of the Faith came to a stop. There was nothing left for it in China but to suffer."

Thus, and it is they themselves who confess it, China had opened all her gates to them up to the day when the missionaries, by order of the Pope, and with little enough gratitude for all the splendid hospitality they had received, began to exercise their arbitrary and autocratic power, condemning the ceremonies that had been adopted by more than four hundred millions of men, in order to replace them with new ceremonies.

It is for such a work that we are to send our children to China to fight those who wish to become once more the masters of their country and their own beliefs!!!

This is what that famous conscience of the Christian army amounts to!

*

*   *

To sum up and make an end of this chimney-cleaning—

In the twentieth century, the Catholic Church is a rich church that has seized upon all the philosophical texts in order to distort them, and Hell prevails. The Word remains.

Nothing of this Word is dead. The Vedas, Brahma, Buddha, Moses, Israel, Greek philosophy, Confucius, the Gospel, all exist.

Without a single tear, without any monopolistic association, Science and Reason have alone preserved the tradition: outside the Church.

From a religious point of view, the Catholic Church no longer exists. It is now too late to save it.

Proud of our conquests, sure of the future, we say, "Halt!" to this cruel and artificial Church. Then we explain our hatred and the reason for this hatred.

The missionary is no longer a man, a conscience. He is a corpse, in the hands of a confraternity, without family, without love, without any of the sentiments that are dear to us.

They say to him, "Kill!"—and he kills. It is God who wills it!

"Seize that region,"—and he seizes it.

"Seize that inheritance,"—and he seizes it.

Your wealth? There is not a square inch of land that you have not extorted from the faithful by the promise of heaven, obliging them to give you the fruits of everything that is sold, even the fruits of prostitution. Poor divers who, braving the sharks, seek for pearls in the depths of the sea. A sign of the cross is all they get for it.

We understand your artifices, gentlemen.

The modern man does not like filth, and the missionary who has sanctified lousiness generally finds himself called Lousy-beard.

Emasculated, in a sense, by his vow of chastity, he offers us the distressing spectacle of a man deformed and impotent or engaged in a stupid and useless struggle with the sacred needs of the flesh, a struggle which, seven times out of ten, leads him to sodomy, the gallows or prison.

Man loves woman, if he has understood what a mother is.

Man loves woman, if he has understood what it is to love a child.

Love thy neighbour!

With sadness and disgust as well I see them passing, this procession of unclean, unhealthy virgins, the Good Sisters, forcibly driven, either by poverty or by the superstition of society, to enter the service of an invading power.

That a mother? . . . *That* a daughter? . . . Never!

And as an artist, a lover of beauty and beautiful harmonies, I exclaim, "*That* a woman? Oh, no!"

Brains unfitted for intellectual quests, having no consciousness of life save as eating and drinking, with no real aim except to obey a rule, covered with a mantle of hypocrisy that is worn with contempt by other male virgins.

Admitting that the police are slanderous, and all those stories, too, richly documented as they are—the condition of the convents in the days of Joan, the monks' prostitute, who became Joan the Pope; the story of Diderot's nun at the time of the Revolution; the discovery of all those corpses of infants, slain at their birth, when the earth in the gardens of certain ancient women's convents was dug up,—admitting that all these are slanders pure and simple, there remains none the less a state of things that is unnatural, cruel and consequently inhuman.

Away with that sentimentality which is the mask of sentiment, that false respect for the cloth!

Take a close look at the Sisters in the colonial hospitals, and those who direct them, the males. They usually require more people to wait on them than the sick people. Beside a patient's bed they seem mere busybodies, though some of them, of course, are good-hearted country girls, capable (at best) of exciting compassion, who now and then give the soldiers cakes for coming to mass. As for the males, gathered together from every nation (French missions!) they are out looking for little Chinese boys, collecting money to repair and keep up the churches, and getting subscriptions for their publication, "La Propagation de la Foi." In this publication you read: "X. . . . 50 francs, for a piece of work successfully done"!!

Edifying, as you see, and this gives us an idea of the grandeur of the Church.

*

*   *

Schools and scholars.

Paul studies Rembrandt. Henri studies Paul. Bonnat studies Henri. You see the sequence.

A caricature by Daumier: out in the sun, some painters are lined up.

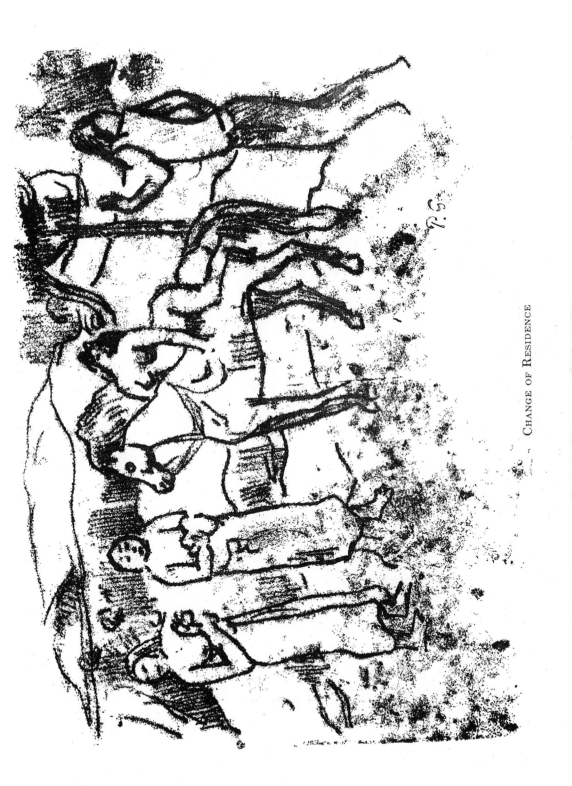

CHANGE OF RESIDENCE

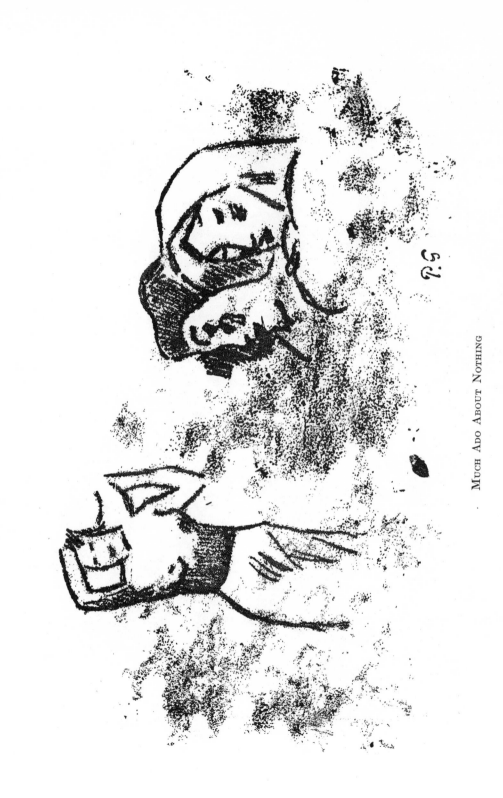

MUCH ADO ABOUT NOTHING

The first is copying nature, the second is copying the first, the third is copying the second. . . . You see the sequence.

A tracing, a tracing of a tracing . . . and one signs.

Nature is less indulgent. After the mule comes nothing.

Paul economizes but dies of hunger. His brother Henri does not economize but dies of indigestion. Which is the wiser, Jean who weeps or Jean who laughs?

*
*   *

He and she loved each other with a tender love, and this went on as long as possible. Then the day came when the lover, the less ingenuous of the two, weary of it, his passion cold, perceived that his beloved was really a hideous ghoul.

Ghouls do not like to have people cast them off.

He, the Abbé Combes, was minded one fine day, bowing to the will of the people, to inform his old sweetheart of some of the details of this will.

Several bullies, obstinate as Bretons always are, appointed to guard the beauty, made ready to defend their soup-kettle—the gratitude of the belly, assuredly. They got together all the night-soil and the ordure of the sisters and flooded the Abbé's messengers with these perfumes of theirs. Drive away filth and it comes back at a gallop.

It was desolating; through the whole countryside they wept, they swore.

Brittany and Vendée were on the point of rising; it was not going to be the chamber-pot this time but the cannon. Alas, three times alas! *Non bis in idem.*

But do not be too sure. . . . The army. . . . The Christian conscience. . . .

You wanted to vent your spite on your old sweetheart, the ghoul you used to love so much; and it was within a hair's-breadth of happening. You did not know that in the army there are several kinds of conscience. A conscience that permits, even commands one to kill without pity men, defenceless women, even children, when they are communists. Another conscience that forbids one to arrest bullies who empty chamber-pots on the heads of gendarmes.

*
*   *

They are all ready to set off for China to massacre the Chinese, who are unwilling to allow themselves to be run by the Christians.

This good France, so generous and so chivalrous, is always ready to set off to war in order to help the English sell their opium; and then to set off to war again to sell the Old and New Testaments.

The Pope, who has nothing left but this stupid France to support his missions, does not want to be angry. He says, "You may demand divorce, but our principles do not authorize it. On principle we do not recognize divorce."

He is a sly one, our Holy Father, little Leo; there is no one slyer.

To those who ask him to make concessions, in order to keep up with the times, he invariably replies, "Concessions! that would be the death of us! We need time. We must preserve our wealth."

And in order to gain time he makes up a few dogmas.

The photograph of the Holy Shroud, when dipped in the water of Lourdes, yields hundreds of prints, by means of radiation, no doubt, like the body of Our Lord Jesus Christ. They expect very soon to start a great subscription in the Marquesas to purchase one of these extraordinary specimens. The piastres are going to hum!

The natives, who take me for a scholar, come to me every day to ask for information. What can I say to them? I should have to take up again the whole study of clerical chemistry and at my age I lack the energy for that.

I say to them, "Ask the sergeant; he is the boss."

Another fellow who has a conscience!!—like india-rubber. You should see how fine he looks when he says, "My duty." And how important when he says, "My dear fellow, I have just slept with a virgin." . . . . It is true that the next month, at the hospital, the major says: "What's all this? Give him some proto-iodine of mercury." These little virgins, the kind Pissarro paints, are dealers in poison.

You are going to say, my Parisian reader, that I am pulling your leg about the gendarmes. Come to the colonies, especially the Marquesas, and you will see if I am pulling your leg. If you have any influence, it will be better still if you have a few words with the minister.

But I have not finished with this subject. I shall be talking to you about it again.

*

*   *

I forgot, a moment ago, when I was speaking to you about my childhood in Lima, to tell you something that illustrates the pride of the Spanish. It may interest you.

In the old days there was a cemetery in Lima in the Indian style: rows of pigeon-holes, with coffins in these pigeon-holes; inscriptions of all sorts. A French business man, M. Maury, took it into his head to look up the rich families and suggest that they should have tombs of sculptured marble. It succeeded marvelously. This one was a general, that one a great captain, etc. . . . all heroes. He had armed himself for the undertaking with several photographs of sculptured tombs in Italy. It was a dazzling success. For several years ships kept arriving filled with marbles sculptured in Italy for a very low price and which made a very good effect.

If you go to Lima now you will see a cemetery that is unlike any other and you will find out how much heroism there is in that country.

Old Maury made an immense fortune from this. His story, simple as it is, deserves to be told.

A great business house at Bordeaux once had on its hands a very large transaction which it considered as good as lost. In this house there was a young clerk—it was young Maury, who had been noticed as a boy of exceptional intelligence.

They sent this young man to Lima with full authority to call in their debts, and agreed to pay him a certain percentage of what was secured, supposing it would not amount to much. They were mistaken, for young Maury set about it so well that he saved almost the whole amount.

After this, he found himself in control of a very pretty capital and in touch with business in Lima, and he asked for nothing better than to stay. He began by building a comfortable hotel, then two, then several others; it was he who had made to order, in sections, the dome of carved wood for the church, which had simply to be put together over the old dome. My mother, who had learned to draw at school, made an admirable—that is to say, an atrocious—pen-drawing of this church, with its garden surrounded by iron railings.

As a child I thought this drawing very pretty; my mother had done it; you will surely understand me.

In Paris I saw old Maury again, very old at that time, with his two nieces beside him, his only heirs. He possessed a very beautiful collection of vases (pottery of the Incas) and jewels set in unalloyed gold by the Indians.

What has become of all these things?

My mother also had kept a few Peruvian vases and especially quite a number of figurines in massive silver, just as it comes out of the mines. They all disappeared in the burning of St. Cloud by the Prussians, along with quite a considerable library and almost all of our family papers. Speaking of family papers, when I was married they asked me at the *mairie* for the death certificates of my parents. I possessed only my mother's, which signified enough, for it read, "Madame Gauguin, widow." But the clerk maintained that I could not marry without the certificate of my father's death.

"But doesn't the fact that my mother was the widow Gauguin prove that my father was dead?"

There is nothing more obstinate than a clerk in a *mairie*. Fortunately the mayor was an intelligent man and everything was straightened out.

At the birth of my son, I went to the *mairie* again to declare this birth. When I dictated to the clerk, "A boy named Emil Sause," he wrote, "Emile Sauzé."

It took an indescribable quarter of an hour to get the spelling right. I was a joker who was making fun of the clerks, etc. . . . A little more and I should have been up for a misdemeanour.

As you see, I have never been serious, and you must not be offended by my jocular style.

*

*   *

Old Moo, without any preliminaries, came and installed herself in my house. Being warm, she took off her chemise. She is very thin, and you know I like fat women. Her skin is all wrinkled; think of it, she has been a mother eleven times. Aside from this, she would look better if she were given a coat of whitewash. She has really had eleven children, but if you ask her how many fathers there were she is quite startled. She counts on her fingers, and again on her fingers—a long time. But when she reaches the number 100 her memory goes back on her.

She owns a little land and every day, if one is to believe her, a real true husband offers himself. But she has her eye on what she says.

What does it matter? She lies down and offers what she has, as if she were the most beautiful girl in the world. Nothing more, nothing less. But I do not like thin women.

For the time being I have a headache. It is going to be measles.

The conversation ceases and she goes to sleep.

Then I dare to look at her; there is no doubt that she ought to have a coat of whitewash.

For several nights she comes back. I always have measles when she comes; my chastity depends on it. And besides, I have no fire.

Finally, she comes no more. When they ask her why, she says she cannot stand it, it is so fatiguing. Showing all her fingers, she says, "Yes, like that, every night!"

That is the way bad reputations are made; make no mistake about it.

*

*   *

There was once a time when the only pictures of mine that could be sold were those I had given away.

A good little fellow, to whom I had given thirty, hastened to sell them at Vollard's—after he had copied and studied them. To excuse himself he spread it about that it was I who had stolen all his studies.

Excellent young man!

Never give your pictures away, except to your cook.

Van Gogh had this mania also. Who does not remember the joint that was kept by La Siccatore, that Italian woman who had been a model? Vincent decorated this whole café (Le Tambourin) for nothing.

During my stay at Arles, he told me a rather curious story about it, a story of which I never heard the end. As he was very much in love with La Siccatore, who was still beautiful in spite of her age, he had a good many confidences from her about Pansini.

La Siccatore had a man with her to help run the café. In this café all sorts of suspicious-looking characters used to gather. The manager wanted to have all the confidences of this woman, and one fine day, without rhyme or reason, he flung a glass of beer at Vincent's face which cut him on the cheek. Vincent, all covered with blood, was thrown out of the café.

A gendarme who was passing at this moment said to him, severely, "Move along!"

According to Van Gogh, the whole Pansini affair, as well as many others, was hatched in this place, with the connivance of Siccatore and the lover.

It is worth noticing that nearly all of these establishments are on the best of terms with the police.

From this Pansini case sprang another case, also, according to Vincent, hatched in this famous café, the Prado case.

This man, in order to rob a certain prostitute, murdered her, then her maid, then her little girl, whom he had violated. It was not until long after that the police, wearied by the noise in the papers, found a so-called murderer who had taken refuge in Havana. It was almost impossible to discover the real name of this extraordinary man. A woman was found who accused him of everything the police wished her to accuse him of, although she was not considered an accomplice. No one understood anything about it, the press, the court, or the murderer, who exclaimed, "It is true I am a thief and have committed murder before this, but I am not guilty of this crime."

The case in this respect recalled Balzac's *Ténébreuse Affaire*. What did it matter? The police were bound to have the last word and this man was condemned to death.

I and a friend were informed by a telegram sent to the Café Nouvelle Athénes by a captain of the municipal guard. At half past two in the morning we were on the Place de la Roquette, stamping our feet, for it was extremely cold on that very dark night, awaiting the execution, or at least (what would help to pass the time) the arrival and setting up of the machine. There was not a moment's hope of getting into the little reserved space beside the machine, for it was already full of motionless people, pressed one against another, waiting for morning. At last the hour drew near. A faint gleam that announced the sunrise allowed me to catch a glimpse of the square. There was a great semi-circle round the guillotine, soldiers, the police. On one side the guillotine wagon and the hearse; on the other, the reserved space.

Before the guillotine, in the centre, five mounted gendarmes.

And suddenly the police began brutally pushing all of us who were on foot toward the outer edge of the circle.

Impossible to see, or so little. . . .

The prison gates opened and the guard began to march out. The gendarmes had drawn their sabres and an extraordinary silence at once fell, as if at a word of command; many removed their hats. By themselves, in black, were the special police and the executioner. The executioner's helpers were in blue blouses.

I still wanted to see, and when I want something I am very obstinate. So I dashed across the square (breaking the respectful silence) and, dodging between the two boots of a gendarme, reached the centre. No one dared to move.

Then I saw the guard advancing slowly, and, between the two posts of the guillotine, a hideous head, bent, ravaged, as if mad with terror.

I was mistaken; it was the chaplain. What an extraordinary actor to be able in this way to counterfeit a murderer, anguish!

The murderer, quite small but of a sturdy appearance, had a handsome, proud head; he looked well in spite of the evil appearance of his closely shaven hair and his coarse linen shirt.

The board wavered so that instead of the neck it was the nose that was hit. The man struggled with pain, and two blue-blouses, brutally pushing on his shoulders, brought the neck into its proper place. There was a long minute, and then the knife did its work.

I struggled to see the head lifted out of the box; three times I was pushed back. They went off a few yards to get water in a pail to pour over the head.

One wondered why a tap had not been got ready just beneath the box for this very thing. And I wondered why they had not measured the prisoner so that, by a turn of a screw, the board might have been just the desired distance from the opening that receives the neck of the condemned.

There you have the famous spectacle that gives such satisfaction to society.

Outside one heard cries of "Vive Prado!"

*

*　　　　*

I am drawing on the beach, on the frontier. A gendarme from the Midi, who suspects me of being a spy, says to me, who come from Orleans: "Are you French?"

"Why, certainly."

"That's odd. *Vous n'avez pas l'accent (lakesent) français.*"

Raphael was the pupil of Perugino. Bouguereau also. And Bouguereau writes ecstatically, "Face to face with nature I see nothing but colour."

Raphael doesn't go in for values; in his pictures there is no distance. Ask yourself if he understood values.

In an exhibition on the Boulevard des Italiens I see a strange head. I do not know why something happened inside of me, why I should have heard strange melodies in front of a picture. The head of a doctor, very pale, with eyes that do not look at you, do not see, but listen.

In the catalogue I read, "Wagner, by Renoir."

There are people who say, "Rembrandt and Michael Angelo are coarse; I like Chaplin better."

A very ugly woman says to me, "I don't like Degas because he paints so many ugly women." Then she adds, "Have you seen my portrait in the salon by Gervex?"

A clothed figure by Carolus-Duran is coarse; a nude by Degas is chaste.

But she's bathing in a tub!!

That is just why she's clean.

But you can see the tub, the syringe, the basin!!

Everything just the way it is at home.

Criticism strips things, but that is another matter.

A critic at my house sees some paintings. Greatly perturbed, he asks for my drawings. My drawings? Never! They are my letters, my secrets. The public man—the private man.

You wish to know who I am; my works are not enough for you. Even at this moment, as I write, I am revealing only what I want to reveal. What if you do often see me quite naked; that is no argument. It is the inner man you want to see. . . . Besides, I do not always see myself very well.

Drawing, what is it? Do not look for a lecture from me on this subject. The critic would probably say that it is a number of things done on paper with a pencil, thinking, no doubt, that there one can find out if a man knows how to draw. To know how to draw is not the same thing as to draw well. Does he suspect, this critic, this judge, that to trace the outline of a painted figure results in a drawing totally different in effect? In Rembrandt's "Portrait of a Traveller" (Lacazes Gallery) the head appears square. Take an outline of it and you will see that the head is twice as high as it is broad.

I remember the time when the public, sitting in judgment on the drawing of the cartoons of Puvis de Chavannes, affirmed, even while granting that Puvis had great gifts of composition, that he did not know how to draw. There was a sensation when one fine day he gave an exhibition at Durand-Ruel's, consisting exclusively of studies in black crayon on a red ground.

"Well, well," said this charming public. "Puvis knows how to draw *like everybody else*. He knows anatomy, proportions, and all the rest of it. But then why doesn't he know how to draw in his paintings?" In a crowd there is always someone who is cleverer than the others, and this clever fel-

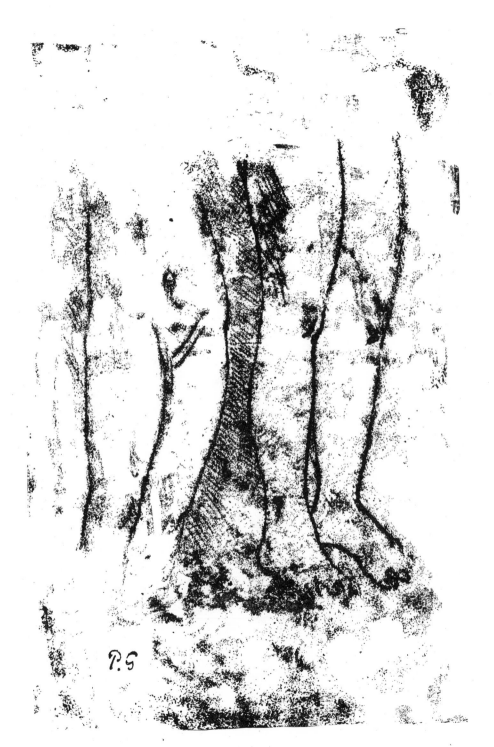

STUDY

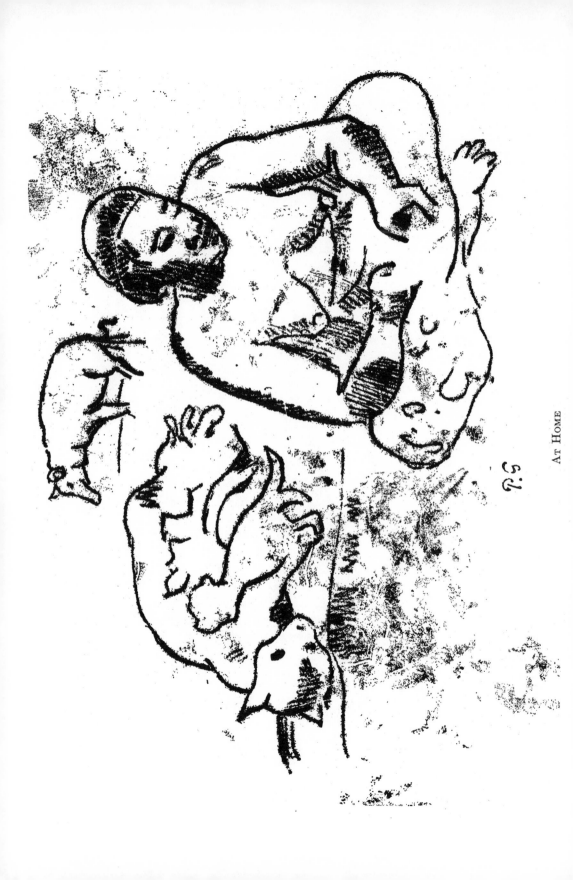

low said, "Can't you see that Puvis is making fun of you? . . . He is another one who wants to be original and not like all the others."

My God, what is to become of us!

That is probably what this critic wished to find out when he asked for my drawings. He said to himself, "We'll see, now, if he knows how to draw." He needn't worry about that, I shall enlighten him. I have never known how to make what they call a proper drawing,—or a bonnet either, or a roll of bread. It always seems to me that there is something lacking —Colour.

Before me is the figure of a Tahitian woman. . . . The white paper troubles me.

Carolus-Duran complains of the Impressionists, of their palette especially. "It is so simple," he says. "Look at Velasquez. A black, a white." As simple as that, the blacks and whites of Velasquez?

I like to listen to such people. On those terrible days when one thinks oneself good for nothing and throws away one's brushes, one remembers them, and hope is born again.

*
*   *

The true ambassadors are those who have not too much confidence in their own intelligence, who reply evasively, who know how to dress and receive.

The same thing seems to be true of the guardians of the Louvre. And yet, and yet, could we not find better ones?

I am speaking to you of many things, in spite of my promise to talk about the Marquesas. It is rather treacherous for me to lure you on in the hope that you are going to get something quite different from what you get in Paris. But you must forgive me; I myself was taken in. Here I am, let us swallow the pill. My brush must make up for it. There are indeed some superb mountains that I could describe to you, more or less untruthfully, but I should have to have the talent for description as well as innumerable adjectives which I do not know but which are so familiar to Pierre Loti.

Many things that are strange and picturesque existed here once, but there are no traces of them left today; everything has vanished. Day by day the race vanishes, decimated by the European diseases,—even measles, which attacks the grown people here. The chicanery of the Administration, the irregularities of the mails, the taxes that crush the colony, render all trade impossible. As a result, the traders are packing up.

There is nothing to say except to talk about women and sleep with them.

Not ripe, almost ripe, quite ripe.

There is so much prostitution that it does not exist. We call it that, but they do not think of it as that.

One only knows a thing by its contrary, and the contrary does not exist.

A rascal of a judge in the Marquesas. . . . A young girl came to complain that twelve men had just violated her, without paying her.

"That's frightful!" exclaimed the judge, and at once he became the thirteenth. But he paid. "You understand, little one, that I cannot judge this case now."

This same judge, when the gendarme was absent, received a young girl, a child really, who had come to get her certificate on leaving school, stating that she was "Fitted for . . ."

"That's all right," our judge said to her; "now give me the first try." And he deflowered her. The card was now signed.

Many such details, often smutty ones, will give you a better understanding of the Marquesas than the tourists get. Tourists today see so little.

The island of Taoata has just been ravaged by a frightful tidal wave which has torn up enormous blocks of coral and many shells for the collectors.

Out of the coral they will make lime. The whalers, who are very clever seamen, observing that their barometers were behaving in extraordinary ways, foresaw the disaster and set out, not without leaving some very pretty presents for the police. Some demijohns of wine. . . . For shame! . . . Presents with bills!!

"What can you expect?" say the captains. "Smugglers have to keep on the right side of the gendarmes."

This requires no comment.

The worst suffering is always the last.

After the morning coffee, the sexes, which have been together at night, separate in the temple: a necessary formality to enable the soul to shake off the matter that subjugates it.

90

After the bath, the holy-water basin; body and soul are cleansed. The prayer goes up, "Lord, give us this day our daily bread."
Business is business.

At the creamery, I am eating a meat-patty with cabbage. My neighbour, an Englishman, asks me what it is called. "Qu'est ce que tu dis?" say I. The waiter passes, and the young man asks for a *Qu'est-ce-que-tu-dis*.
I never knew I was such a wit.

*
*   *

Effects—they exist and have their good points. They are very effective! You should not abuse them, however, unless you are trying to avoid drawing and colour.

When I am in doubt about spelling my handwriting becomes illegible. How many people use this stratagem in painting—when the drawing and the colour embarrass them.

In Japanese art there are no values. Well, all the better! It all depends on the point of view from which one judges. In a shooting-gallery the perspective is itself decoration. · One can get along without hangings or mural paintings. One ought always to feel the wall.

*
*   *

No more painting, no more literature; the time has come to talk of arms. It happens that we have here now a real *gendarme*. . . . You understand. . . . He comes from Joinville le Pont!! He's a terrible swashbuckler. Joinville represents, in a way, the prix de Rome of physical exercises.

There's a good deal in its teaching to be taken or left. For my own personal part, I should leave it.

The fencing-masters turned out at Joinville le Pont are generally very expert fellows, expert in the art of the cudgel blow. They are certainly very able, but they are acrobats and usually cannot do much with their pupils.

The saying goes, Have a good hand, and you will touch sometimes. Have a good hand and good legs and you will touch often. Add a good head, and you will always touch.

A good head, that is what they do not give you at Joinville. They teach without discernment there.

The game of foils consists in making use of two movements; the others are developed from them or are supplementary.

A backward and forward movement, and a turning movement.

In the attack, they are called, *One*, *two*, *three* and *double* . . .

In the defence, they are called *Opposition* and *counter*.

Simple as they are, these movements are capable of an enormous number of combinations. To know them well is to be skilful already.

The regimental fencing-master, who excels in tiring you out, keeps you doing one, two, three and double for a whole year; at the end, when the pupil wishes to make the least little attack, he loses his head. "What shall I do?" he wonders, "Come, one, two . . ." He attacks, he disengages; his adversary takes the counter. It doesn't work. Naturally! . . . Your movements ought to correspond with the parade.

It is essential, therefore, for the instructor to make the pupil really understand by giving him his lesson slowly and thwarting by his parade the movement commanded. Thus, for example, he gives the command one, two, but instead of an opposition he parries gently with a counter, so that the pupil attentively follows the parade and acts accordingly. Now in regard to execution, they have a principle at Joinville le Pont which they will not give up: Throw your arm out and lunge. But this makes it impossible for the adversary to misjudge the distance; if he is attentive to the movement of the knee, he is constantly forewarned.

Good civilian fencing-masters do quite differently. The arm is stretched out gradually and the feint, which is often useless, is only incidental.

We are willing to be corrected if we must be, but we distinctly maintain that one should use one's arms according to the way in which one is built.

Thus, for example, as I have a weak wrist and a delicate hand, I accustomed myself to use the muscles of the arm, with all the strength concentrated in the small of the arm.

As I have a very large chest and did not take up the practice of arms until very late, it was impossible for me, except with the greatest discomfort, to hold myself according to regulations, almost covered on the two lines. So without any discomfort, with my chest unprotected, I accustomed myself to offer only a single line to my adversary, always opening the engagement in tierce (today they say in *sixte*).

I remember a certain first-class fencing-master at the Salle Hiacinte in Paris. This instructor had arms and especially legs that were very small, and he was in the habit of using his legs as if he had little wheels under the balls of his feet. He never lunged, but by means of a series of little steps, now forward, now back, he would be out of reach or directly upon you at once. The head . . . always the head! You have a strong wrist, then wear your adversary out with attacks, press him hard with sustained energy. But if your hand is weak, let it skilfully parry all attacks, without attacking itself. In fencing there are no dogmas, any more than there are secret thrusts.

During my stay at Pont-Aven, the harbour-master and fish-warden was a Breton of the place, a retired sailor who was a fencing-master with a diploma from this famous school of Joinville le Pont. With his help, we opened a little fencing-school which, in spite of the low charges, brought him a little income that gave him great satisfaction. He was a fine old boy and a pretty good fencer, but not intelligent either as a fencer or as an instructor. He really had no understanding of the science of arms. All he knew he had got through stubbornness and endless practice.

From the first day, I saw that the poor man had very short legs, so I, who am tall and long-legged, amused myself between whiles making him mistake his distances, the result being that, in spite of his skill of hand, he was always inches away from his mark. I talked to him about it, but I might as well have been speaking Hebrew. Fortunately the old boy was not proud, and for a while I became his instructor in all sorts of ways. I gave him lessons in the manner I have described above, that is, opposing the pupil, during the lesson, with parades different from those that had been announced.

Before long, we had an excellent master and the pupils made rapid progress.

To mistake distances. It is evident that if you are going to attack, you must, without letting anyone perceive it, come, with your elbows to your body, as close to your adversary as possible, by an extension of the arm and a certain trick of stepping. In this way, the arm extending stealthily, that is to say, in proportion to its movements, touches its mark without the help of the legs. In the same way, in the opposite case, your arm ought to be extended, you ought to lean slightly forward; then you have the advantage of the whole length of your arm and a certain distance which you gain in resuming the upright position.

The military fencing-masters teach you not to attack until very late, that is to say, when the pupil is discouraged. . . . A civilian master, almost at the beginning, ends the lesson with a lesson in attack, allowing certain openings, making certain mistakes, all this very slowly, so that in no case does the pupil form the habit of muffing. What, I have made an attack and you have not disengaged? What, I have parried with an opposition and you have tried to double? And so on. In this way the pupil, interested from the very beginning, learns the science of arms and is accustomed from the first to apply the lesson in an attack, and makes very rapid progress, without, however, tiring himself out as if he were an acrobat.

The various fencing-matches that take place in Paris every year are the proof of what I have just been saying, for one sees fencing-masters beaten by civilians who have had ten times less practice than they.

The head, it is always the head.   .   .   .

Our excellent master at Pont-Aven was very much astonished when one fine autumn day there arrived at the fencing-school a pair of swords, a present from an American pupil who had well-lined pockets.

In a match with the professor, I showed him that this again was quite a different game.

Certainly one must always begin the study of arms with foils; that is the best foundation. But one has to apply this knowledge quite differently in a duel. In a duel, the question is not one of correctly touching certain specified spots; here everything counts. One must consider that on the field dangerous strokes are also dangerous for oneself.

A man who parries well and returns cleverly is a fine swordsman.

There is no regular position; it is the adversary who indicates to us the position we ought to assume. Everything is unforeseen, everything is irregular. In a way, it is a game of checkers. The victory is to him who deceives the other and is the last to be tired out. Beware of having your nails underneath, for a strong blow will surely disarm you. Your arm should be extended slowly, and in the line of tierce; otherwise a binding of the blade is to be feared. The contrary is true if your adversary is left-handed.

Study your adversary carefully, find out what are his favourite parades, unless he is too clever and plays the game they play at school—evens and odds. In this case, you must have very irregular and unexpected movements in order to make your adversary believe you are about to do something quite different from what you intend.

I could write at length on this subject, but I hope the reader has sufficiently understood.

Finally, if you have to do with an adversary who clearly out-matches you, guard yourself well and, at the least forward movement on his part, present your arm to his point. Honour is satisfied and you get off with a trifling wound.

On the other hand; if you have before you someone who has never fenced, take care, he is dangerous. He uses a sword simply as he does a stick, slashing up and down. Do not hesitate, make the counterpoint, and a blow on the head or in the face will properly settle him for you.

I have met many braggarts in my life, especially on trips to the colonies. You have only to talk with fellows like this for a few moments to know how to deal with them. Thus a little solicitor, whom I have already introduced to you, told me one day that he was a terrible fellow, as he had spent fifteen years in a fencing-school—he, a little shrimp whose sex and species it would have been hard to specify!

I seized the opportunity, one day when I had been asked to lunch with him on a certain warship, to bring the conversation around to this subject. I said to him, "I have not spent fifteen years in a fencing-school, but I'll wager you a hundred francs and give you eight to ten." Naturally he did not take me up.

In the regiment, the officers do not go to the fencing-school, they prefer going to the club to play cards. As for the soldiers, it is a bore all round, for them and the master alike. Some show a turn for it; they are made assistant masters.

In military training they make use of the body but never of the head.

I have often had occasion to cross swords with these assistant masters; they are all of them unintelligent hacks.

It is almost the same thing at school. You must have some knowledge of fencing to enter St. Cyr, and the master tries to earn his money as peacefully as he can.

I remember those days. We had as our master the famous Grisier, who used to send us his assistant. (I do not remember his name, but he must still be alive, for he has a fencing-school in Paris.) This assistant was celebrated for his thrusts.

Old Grisier used to come sometimes, engage with the foil in his right hand, and with his left hand manage to give us a light tap on the cheek. I have received them. It was really an honour he did us, calling it the Grisier thrust. He had been the Czar of Russia's fencing-master.

I have talked enough about fencing, and you must excuse me. It is all because of this famous gendarme who comes from Joinville le Pont. But I am not going to let you off, just the same. I am going to bore you now with a little lesson in boxing. Another chance for a little boasting!

I did not get my first lessons in boxing in early youth. My master was an amateur, a painter at Pont-Aven named Bouffard. Although only an amateur, he was fairly able. I have kept it up since, and it has been of use to me on several occasions, even when it has only served to give me assurance. But I am speaking of English boxing; at Joinville le Pont they practise what they call French boxing, or *savate*. When I was a sailor, I practised *savate* for the fun of the thing.

Charlemont the younger, the present-day champion of French boxing, has created a real art of boxing which is not exclusively *savate*. Very, very different from this is the school of Joinville le Pont. Imperfect as it is, the English school is the better.

The boxing at Joinville le Pont has no value except for a very agile man, an acrobat, very skilful and extremely strong. Otherwise it is a real danger that quickly puts you at the mercy of a very ordinary English boxer.

That is my whole lesson in boxing; it consists in putting you on your guard against the school of Joinville. If you should have a fancy to take it up, you must have agile legs, practise every day, give up all reading and become a *brute*.

*
*   *

Giving is not the same thing as knowing how to give. To know how to give one must know how to receive.

They say one must know how to obey in order to know how to command. That is not quite exact. Witness the kings. Witness the police also. As spiritless as valets, they know how to obey; do they know how to command? Great God, no! And yet, they love to command; they call this compensating themselves or avenging themselves.

"I am the boss!!"

At home I dress in a shirt; in my studio in a blouse; at night, in company, in evening clothes.

In that blind alley, rather like the Cour des Miracles, the Impasse Frenier, opening on the Rue des Fourneaux. Five o'clock in the morning. I am not asleep and I hear Mother Fourel, the carter's wife, screaming, "Help! my husband has hung himself!"

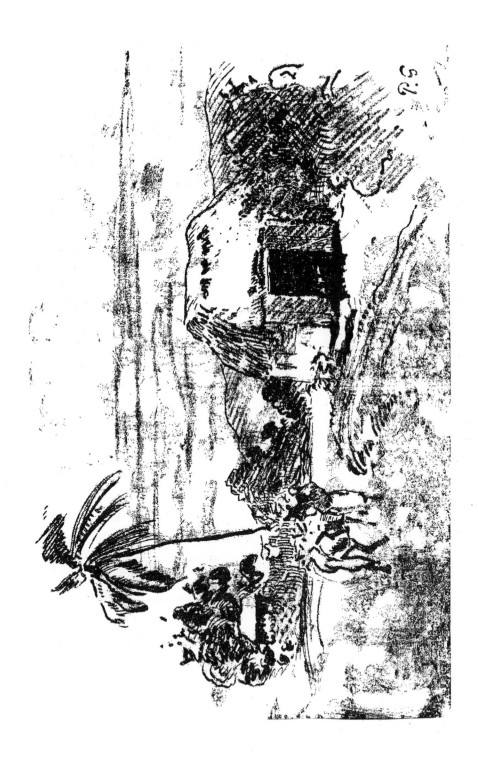

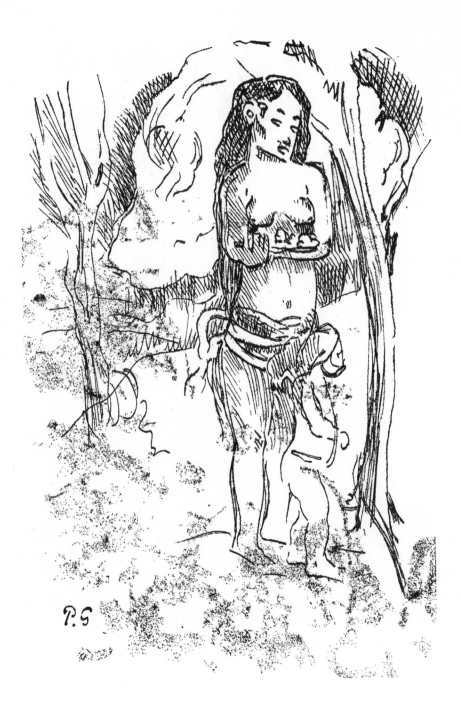

I leap out of bed, pull on a pair of trousers (the proprieties!) grab a knife downstairs and cut the rope. The man is dead, still warm, still burning. I want to carry him to a bed. Stop! we must wait for the police.

On the other side my house overhangs fifteen yards of market-gardeners' beds.

"Have you a cantaloup?" I call to the gardener.

Certainly, a good ripe one, and at breakfast I eat my melon without a thought of the man who has hung himself. There is good in life, as you see. Beside the poison there is the antidote. And in the evening, in my dress coat, expecting to thrill the company, I relate the story. Smiling, quite unconcerned, they all ask me for pieces of the rope with which he hung himself.

One story leads to another. I recall an evening once when I had been drinking a little and was coming home, about midnight, along a street in Havre. At that time I was a sailor on a merchant ship. I nearly broke my nose against a half-open window-shutter that stuck out into the street.

"Pig!" I shouted, and I gave the shutter a blow. It would not close. For a good reason; there was a man hanging there who wouldn't let it. This time I did not cut him down but went on my way (I had drunk a little too much), saying to myself over and over in a loud voice: "The pig! The hell of a lot he cares about passers-by. It was enough to break your face!" Happy are those who are always *comme il faut*.

The stories one hears in Oceania are many and interesting. Here is one that is not my own, as it happened to someone else; but I can guarantee it.

On my first trip as a pilot's apprentice on the *Luzitano*, bound for Rio de Janiero, it was my duty to stand watch at night with the lieutenant. He told me the following.

He had been a cabin-boy on a little ship that made long voyages in Oceania with cargoes of all sorts of cheap goods. One fine morning, while he was washing the deck, he fell into the sea without anyone's noticing it. He did not let go of his broom, and thanks to this broom the boy kept up for forty-eight hours in the ocean. By an extraordinary chance a ship happened to pass and saved him. Then, some time later, as this ship had put in at a hospitable little island, our cabin-boy went for a walk and stayed a little too long. So he remained for good and all.

Our little cabin-boy pleased everybody, so there he was settled, with nothing to do, forced to lose his virginity on the spot, fed, lodged, petted and flattered in every way. He was very happy. This lasted two years;

then one fine morning another ship happened to be passing and our young man wanted to go back to France.

"My God, what a fool I was," he said to me. "Here I am now obliged to fight my way against wind and wave. . . . And I was so happy!!"

Living among the savages is all very well, but there is such a thing as Homesickness.

If age but could,—that doesn't matter.
If youth but knew.—That is what matters.
I have never done so well as when I wanted to do ill.
All this is said and written for people who have no morals.
One day I was treacherously taken to call on a respectable family (my sister was with me) where they talked about nothing but family duties and household virtues. It was like a flash of lightning for me; *unmistakably* I saw it was a marriage-trap. There is nothing so terrible as virtue.

A widow trots out her three daughters. Look at the mother; you will see what the daughters are going to become. That is not alluring.

Today a father should say to his future son-in-law:
"Have you had syphilis?"
"No. . . ."
"Very well, but you can't have my daughter then, for that means you are subject to the disease and might contaminate her."

There are necessities one has to swallow. Swallow is a hard word; let us say, to which one must resign oneself.

Old men have no teeth left; old wolves have famous ones.
A woman never becomes really good till she becomes a grandmother. In Oceania. . . . I do not say this of you, Ladies of the Metropolis. If not from conviction, through politeness.
Turlututu, mon chapeau pointu!

*

*   *

And he said to me, "Every man ought to serve his country."
And I: "Why haven't you served?"
"Oh, that's another story; I am exempt, I come from the colonies."
Patriotism!!
Well, my mind has set off on a journey. We are not in Oceania any longer but in Africa, that good continent which everybody wants to share,

or rather to quarrel over, and which is so favourable to the adventurous heroes who come to trade, that land where they cut people's throats under the pretext of spreading civilization. When they are tired of firing at rabbits they fire at the blacks. The Boers fire at the blacks, saying: "Get out of here and make room for me." Heaven knows, the English do no worse; they only like to amuse themselves with a little sentiment. They used to sell slaves; now it is forbidden. No, I am only coughing; go and see for yourselves.

Well, there are many Arabic manuscripts in Africa to instruct us. So I have been told and I believed it. I have listened with the greatest attention. Do as I did, if you want to know what they say.

It is not all sand in the desert; here and there are smiling landscapes and clove-trees with their noses in the air.

On a day which the Arabic manuscript does not specify for us, a lion and an ass happened to meet. "My compliments!" exclaimed Master Ass at once, and our proud king of the desert replied, "I accept them with pleasure."

The lion, having no great love for water, said to the ass, as they were approaching a river, "Are you strong enough to carry me across the river on your back? It would certainly save me from a case of bronchitis."

Our ass, happy to please so dangerous a companion, was glad to place himself at his disposal, when . . . all at once he felt his rump wickedly torn. He began to bray loudly, "My God! What's that?"

"Oh, nothing," answered the lion; "it's my claw."

Further on they came to a little hill and our ass turned to his king of the desert: "Would you be able to run up that little hill with me on your back?"

Sparing of words, the Arabic manuscript only tells us that the lion easily accomplished the task, when . . . all at once the lion felt an extraordinary instrument, a natural arm, a stake undoubtedly, cruelly perforating his bowels. This time there was a roar, "My God! What's that?"

And our ass, with that jovial air peculiar to his species, said, "Oh, nothing, that is my claw!"

There are two sorts of claws, and the most terrible is not the one you would think. One must not confuse it with the ass's kick. The Arabic philosopher means something quite different.

*

*   *

"Mordioux! Cap des Dioux!" One hand pulling the moustache, the other on the sword-hilt.

Today—"Wha-a-t!" and one spits on one's hands.

And they say we are evolving!

I had a "Mardi Gras in Spain" by Goya. I copied it but I changed it, putting the people in evening clothes and top-hats. Not as good but more of a masquerade.

Before me is an old bamboo; it was carved by a savage. It is a geometrical figure, the square of the hypotenuse. A geometry in a state of shipwreck undoubtedly, and this interests me. I should have liked to know what was going on in the brain of this native artist, but the artist is dead.

I also have a book of travels, full of illustrations—India, China, the Philippines, Tahiti, etc. . . . All the faces, carefully copied with the idea that they are portraits, look like Minerva or Pallas. What a fine thing the School is!

Jean Dollent, in his book *Les Monstres*, has his cook say, "You don't serve turnips with a leg of mutton." And he adds, "The Conservatoire!"

If you have children who are good for nothing, give them a good leathering. That is still the best method of getting them somewhere.

An official here said to me, "Do you know Huysmans? It seems he is a great writer; he has just been decorated."

"Yes, but Huysmans has been decorated as a clerk of the ministry."

And our official, delighted, answers, "Oh, that explains it."

The real glory is to be known by the omnibus conductors.

Old Corot at Ville-d'Avray: "Well, Père Mathieu, does this picture please you?"

"Oh, yes, indeed, the rocks look just the way they do."

The rocks were cows.

In populo veritas.

*

*   *

What is remarkable about the great Revolution is that the leaders were the led. A flock of sheep leading another flock. Everything begins well only to end badly. Marat seems to me the one man who knew what he wanted. Naturally he had to be killed by a woman;—the grain of sand that stops the machine! Can fatality by any chance be conscious? Oh, but then the word has no meaning, or at least I cannot understand it. I was brought up by people who looked on history as teaching, whereas it is all an open question; I have never seen two conclusions about it that agreed. I sincerely hope that if we had a war with England tomorrow, we should not let ourselves be led by a real Maid of Orleans.

I regard the historians as very honest fellows, but how embarrassed they must be when they have to pick and choose out of all that heap. For my part, it seems to me if I consulted history I should do one stupid thing after another. It is certainly true that in politics I am like almost all artists,—I have no understanding of them whatever.

For some time it has simply appeared to me as if all the nations were trying to see which could embrace the other the most. I drink to the health of them all!! . . . the Kings, the Emperors, the Presidents of the Republics. Like a simpleton, I say to myself, "There is something that stinks here."

*

*   *

In a drawing-room, the little ninny of a gentleman who reads all the political papers is gravely holding forth. When he utters the phrase "Triple Alliance" he displays his clenched fist, the symbol of power.

In a corner, an amazed listener asks his neighbour, "Who is that gentleman?"

"He's an attaché, a young fellow who is going far."

If you want to be taken seriously, talk politics, talk about the Triple Alliance, which is so substantial that for thirty years they have been perpetually patching it up.

*

*   *

Zola had his hatreds. Without being a great man like him, one can, it seems to me, have one's hatreds also. Such a one am I.

I hate Denmark profoundly, its climate, its inhabitants.

Oh, there is good in Denmark, undoubtedly. Thus, during the last twenty-five years, while Norway and Sweden have invaded the picture-shows in France in order to copy whatever is being done that looks well, no matter how bad it may be, Denmark, ashamed of the blow it received at the Universal Exposition of 1878, began to reflect and even concentrate on itself. From this has resulted a very personal Danish art which is worthy of serious attention and which I am happy to praise here. It is good to study French art, and that of all the other countries as well, but only so as to be better able to study oneself.

They once played a curious trick upon me in Copenhagen. I, who asked for nothing, was earnestly invited and entreated by a certain gentleman, in the name of an art club, to exhibit my works in a hall *ad hoc*. I allowed myself to be persuaded.

On the day of the opening I set out—but not till the afternoon—to have a glance at it. What was my astonishment, on arriving, to be told that the exhibition had been officially closed at noon.

It was useless to seek for any information whatever; on all sides were closed mouths. I took one leap to the house of the important gentleman who had invited me. This gentleman, the servant told me, had left for the country and would not be back for some time.

As you see, Denmark is a charming land.

It must be admitted, too, that in Denmark they sacrifice a good deal to education, to the sciences, and quite particularly to medicine. The hospital at Copenhagen may be considered one of the finest establishments of the sort, in its importance and especially in its management, which is of the highest order.

Let us grant them this praise, especially since, aside from this, I can see nothing else about them that is not positively baleful. Oh, excuse me, I am forgetting this one other thing, their houses are admirably built and arranged so as to be warm in winter and well-aired in summer, and the city is attractive. It must also be said that receptions in Denmark are usually held in the dining-room, where they have excellent food. It is always excellent, and that helps to pass the time. You must not allow yourself to be too bored by this perpetual sort of conversation: "You come from such a great country, you must find us very slow, we are so small. What do you think of Copenhagen, our museum, etc? It doesn't amount to much?" All this said so that you will say just the contrary—as you assuredly will, out of politeness. Good manners!!!

The museum, to speak of that. Frankly, it has no collection of pictures at all, except for a few examples of the old Danish school, some Meissoniers, and a few landscapes and marines. Let us hope that this has changed today. There is a monument expressly made for it by their great sculptor Thorwaldsen, a Dane who lived and died in Italy. I have seen this and studied it till my head hummed. Greek mythology turned Scandinavian and then, with another dilution, Protestant. Venuses lowering their eyes and modestly draping themselves in damp linen. Nymphs dancing a jig. Yes, gentlemen, dancing a jig; look at their feet.

In Europe they speak of "the great Thorwaldsen," but they have not seen him. The only work that travelers see is his famous lion in Switzerland!! A stuffed Danish dog.

When I say this, I know that in Denmark they will burn sugar in every corner to teach me a lesson for insulting the greatest of Danish sculptors.

Many other things make me hate Denmark, but they are quite special reasons that one has to keep to oneself.

Let me introduce you into a drawing-room such as one rarely sees nowadays, the drawing-room of a count of the highest Danish nobility.

The vast apartment is square. Two enormous panels of German tapestry, specially executed for the family, more wonderful than anything you can imagine. Above the door, two views of Venice by Turner. The furniture of carved wood with the family arms, inlaid tables, old-fashioned draperies. All one marvel of art.

You are introduced and they receive you. You sit down on a red velvet cushion shaped like a snailshell. On the marvelous table is a cover that must have cost a few francs at the Bon Marché. A photograph-album and some flower vases in the same style. Vandals!!!

Beside the drawing-room, a very pretty music-room. The collection of pictures, the portrait of an ancestor by Rembrandt, etc.

This smells of mould; no one ever goes into it.

The family prefers the chapel, where they read the Bible and where everything petrifies you.

I recognize that the Danish system of betrothal has this much to be said for it, it does not pledge you to anything. You change your fiancée as you change your shirt. Then it has all the appearance of love, liberty and morality. You are engaged; you can go for a walk or even a journey; the mantle of the betrothal is there to cover everything. You play with Everything-but-That, which has advantages on both sides; you learn not to forget yourself and commit imprudences. At each betrothal, the bird loses a lot of little feathers that grow again without anyone's noticing it. Very practical, the Danes. . . . Taste them, but do not let yourself become entangled with them. You might repent of it; and remember, the Danish woman is above everything practical. It is a small country, as one understands, and has to be prudent. Even the children are taught to say, "Papa, we've got to have some money—or you can chase yourself, old boy." I have known it all.

I hate the Danes.

Their literature is said to be good. I am not familiar with it. I. remember, however, seeing a play of Brandes—no—yes—I am not sure. It was about a man who, stopping at a hotel while he was travelling, had profited by one of those moments that are so dangerous for a woman. He meets her again later, living peacefully with her husband. The man threatens to break his silence, and the woman resigns herself.

As you see, touching and always new.

I have also seen a performance of *Othello*. The great tragedian Rossi, who was on a tour, played Othello in Italian; the other parts were in Danish. Iago, the villain, was as flexible as the bar of justice, and Desdemona, in spite of all her efforts to simulate a warm-blooded Spanish woman, scarcely reached the zero point (melting ice).

Then I have seen them play Zola's *Pot-Bouille*. There the actors were in their element. Dish-washing, bourgeois clumsiness. The Josserands were perfect, Trublot slightly less so.

Aside from all this, the Danes dance very well; one must suppose that all their talent goes into this. The Danes are not to be judged in Paris but in their homes. With us they are as sweet as sugar; at home they are pure vinegar.

These people have very curious ways of being modest. Thus, in the Sund, the estates adjoin one another, and each one has its own bath-house for dressing and undressing. The road overhangs them.

The women bathe separately and the men too, at their own hours. They bathe naked and it is the rule that the passer-by on the road must see nothing.

I must confess that, being by nature very curious, I broke the rule one day when the wife of one of the ministers was walking into the sea down a gentle slope of beach. I confess, too, that this perfectly white body, naked to the middle of the calves, made a very good effect. Her little daughter, who was following, turned about and, catching sight of me, cried, "Mamma!!"

The mother turned round, frightened, and started back to the bath-house, thus showing me all the front after having shown me the back. I confess that the front again, at a distance, made a very good effect.

It was a great scandal. What! To have looked!!!

On a French beach a Danish girl, having clothed herself in a bathing-costume, according to our custom, and come out of her bath-house, hesitated, modest Dane that she was, to go in bathing with all these men and

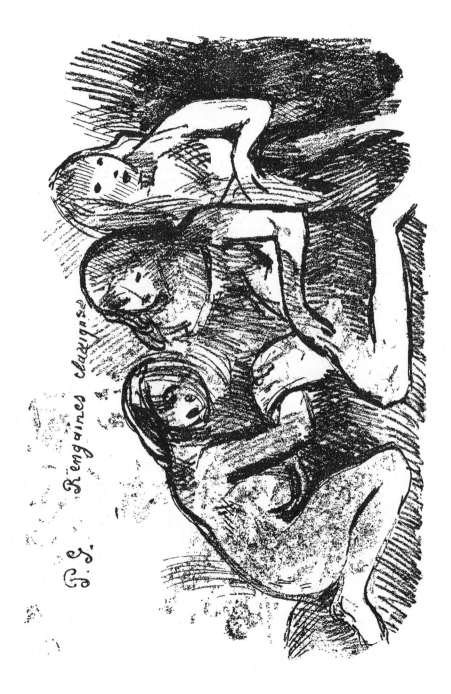

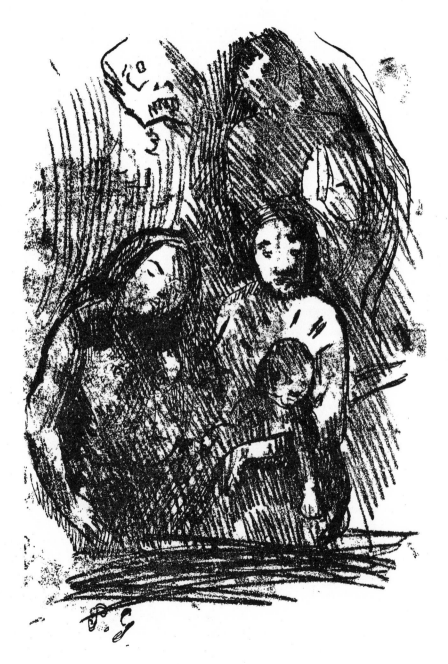

FANTAISIES RELIGIEUSES

women. The woman in charge of the bath-houses, to whom she spoke, replied, "Doesn't Madame see the ocean?" The bathing-master was heard to exclaim: "There's another one showing me her behind when she wouldn't give me her hand with her clothes on!"

Another amusing prude was that young Danish girl whom I saw in a free sculpture atelier, carefully measuring, with an enormous compass, the distance from the model's what-do-you-call-it to his ankle.

The model, who was very cold, behaved himself.

This young Dame took her meals at the creamery opposite, without ever taking off her gloves. One portion, forty centimes, two sous' worth of bread. As you see, wisdom itself, economy and elegance; and above all, she never miscalculated by a tenth of an inch the distance from the what-do-you-call-it to the ankle. She wanted to get it just right; it was the probity of art. She capped it all by winning a medal at the Salon.

*

*   *

My first trip as a pilot's apprentice was on board the *Luzitano* (Havre to Rio de Janiero). A few days before our departure a young man came to me and said, "Is it you who are going to take my place as apprentice? Here's a little package and a letter. Would you be kind enough to see that they reach this address?"

I read, "Madame Aimée, Rua do Ouvidor."

"You will see," said he, "a charming woman to whom I have recommended you in a quite particular fashion. She comes from Bordeaux, as I do."

I will spare you the voyage, reader; that would bore you. I may say, however, that Captain Tombarel was a quadroon and an altogether charming old fellow, that the *Luzitano* was a fine ship of 1200 tons, with excellent accommodations for passengers, and that with a fair wind it made its twelve knots an hour.

It was a very fine passage, without a storm.

As you may imagine, my first thought was to take my little package and the letter to the address indicated. This was a joy. . . .

"How nice of him to have thought of me, and let me take a good look at you, my dear. How handsome you are!" At this time I was quite small; although I was seventeen and a half, I looked fifteen.

In spite of this I had already committed my first sin at Havre, before sailing, and my heart was beating madly. For me it was an absolutely delicious month.

This charming Aimée, in spite of her thirty years, was extremely pretty; she was the leading actress in Offenbach's operas. I can still see her, in her splendid clothes, setting out in her carriage, drawn by a spirited mule.

Everyone paid court to her, but at this moment her acknowledged lover was a son of the Czar of Russia who was a midshipman on the training-ship. He spent so much money that the ship's commander tried to get the French consul to intervene as adroitly as he could.

Our consul got Aimée to come to his office, and awkwardly remonstrated with her. Aimée, not at all put out, began to laugh and said to him, "My dear Consul, it enchants me to hear you talk, and I feel sure you must be a very fine diplomat, but . . . but I feel sure too that when it comes to the breeches-end you know nothing at all."

And she went out singing, "Tell me, Venus, what pleasure do you find in overthrowing my virtue thus?"

Aimée overthrew my virtue. The soil was propitious, I dare say, for I became a great rascal.

On the return voyage, we had several passengers, among others, a fine, fat Prussian woman. It was the captain's turn to be smitten, but fiercely as he burned he burned in vain. This Prussian dame and I had found a charming nest in the room where the sails were stored, the door of which opened into the cabin near the companion-way.

An astonishing liar, I told her all manner of absurdities, and the Prussian dame, who was deeply smitten, wanted to see me again in Paris. I gave her as my address *La Farcy, rue Joubert.*

It was very bad of me and I felt remorse for some time afterwards, but I could not send her to my mother's house.

I do not wish to make myself out as either better or worse than I am. At eighteen you have all sorts of seeds in you.

*
*   *

Roujon, man of letters, Director of the Beaux-Arts.

An audience is granted me and I am introduced.

In this same director's office I had been introduced two years before, with Ary Renan, before I went off to study in Tahiti; to facilitate my studies, the Minister of Public Instruction had given me a mission. It was in this director's office that they had said to me, "No salary goes with this mission; but, as our custom is, and as we have done before, in the case of the painter Dumoulin's mission in Japan, we shall indemnify you on your return by making some purchases. You may count upon us, Monsieur Gauguin; when you come back, write to us and we shall send you the expenses of the trip."

Words! words!

Here I am, then, before the august Roujon, Director of the Beaux-Arts. He says to me, deliciously enough: "I do not feel able to encourage your art. It revolts me and I do not understand it. Your art is too revolutionary not to cause a scandal in *our* Beaux-Arts, of which I am the Director, sustained by the inspectors."

The curtain stirred and I thought I saw Bouguereau, that other director. . . . (Who knows? perhaps I did.) . . . He was certainly not there, but I have a vagabond imagination, and for me he was.

What, I a revolutionary! I who adore and respect Raphael!

What is a revolutionary art? In what epoch does revolution cease?

Yes, not to submit to a Bouguereau or a Roujon constitutes a revolution, so then and there I confess to being the Blanqui of painting.

And this excellent Director of the Beaux-Arts (centre right) also says to me, in regard to the promises of his predecessor, "Have you a written agreement?"

Are the directors of the Beaux-Arts lower than the humblest mortals of the slums of Paris, that their word, even before witnesses, has no value without their signature?

However little sense one may have of human dignity, there is nothing left in such cases but to retire; which is what I immediately did, no richer than I was before.

One year after my departure for Tahiti (my second trip) this very amiable and delicate director, having learned from some simple soul, no doubt, who, though an admirer of mine, still believed in good deeds, that I was in Tahiti, confined to my bed with illness and in the extremest poverty, sent me officially the sum of two hundred francs, "by way of encouragement."

As you may imagine, the two hundred francs were returned to the director.

You are in debt to someone and you say to him, "Come, here's a little sum of which I *make you a present* by way of encouragement. . . ."

*

*   *

I always meant to hate Bouguereau, but it turned into indifference. Then once I found myself smiling at him. It was when I went to old Louis' establishment in Arles and was very proudly shown into his special salon. As an artist, I ought to be a good judge, he said.

In this salon were two of Goupil's most beautiful prizes, a Madonna by Bouguereau and its twin sister, a Venus by the same painter. In this instance old Louis had shown himself a man of genius. Like the magnificent brothel-keeper he was, he had understood the far from revolutionary art of Bouguereau and just where it belonged.

*
*   *

Cabanel! That's another matter.

I hated him during his life-time, I hated him after his death, and I shall hate him till I die myself. This is why.

As a young man, on a trip to the Midi, I visited the famous museum at Montpellier which M. Brias had built and given with its entire collection. It is unnecessary to say who this famous Brias was, this painter and friend of painters, the despair of Raoul de St. Victor.

The main part of this museum contained a very beautiful collection of Italian masters, Giotto, Raphael, etc. . . . In the middle room were some Millets and bronzes by Barye. From this one entered a very large room, a third of which was raised several steps above the rest. Here was Brias' personal collection, that is to say, his selection of what were then the revolutionary painters. O Roujon!

There were portraits of Brias by himself, by Courbet, by Delacroix and others. . . . A number of Courbet's canvasses, among them his great picture of the bathers. . . . A number of studies and sketches by Delacroix for his great decorations, among others "Daniel in the Lions' Den." . . . A number of Corots, Tassaerts, etc. . . . A masterly canvas by Chardin, a large portrait of a noble lady seated before a table, embroidering tapestry. The whole collection, revolutionary as it was, was for me a source of joy, till suddenly my eye fastened on a spot that was entirely out of harmony, a little canvas showing the head of a young man, a pretty boy, as pretty as a hair-dresser. Stupidity and fatuity! Cabanel, painted by himself.

I have forgotten many of these names. There were several things by Ingres, among others a famous picture the name of which . . . my memory has gone back on me . . . I have forgotten. It is a young king, lying in bed, about to die with his secret. In the alcove is the physician, with his hand placed over the young man's heart. Some young maid-servants are filing past, and at the sight of one of them his heart leaps. It is Ingres at his best.

A good many years later I returned, in Vincent's company, and visited this museum again. What a change! Most of the old pictures had vanished, and everywhere their places were filled with—"Acquired by the State, 3rd Medal."

Cabanel and his whole school had invaded the museum.

You must know that Cabanel came from Montpellier.

*

*   *

I hate nullity, the half-way.

In the arms of the beloved who says to me, "Ah, my handsome Rolla, you are killing me!" I do not want to be obliged to say, "No, I'm not in form this evening."

I must have everything. I cannot conquer everything but I will to do so.

Let me get my breath and cry once more:

"Spend yourself, spend yourself again! Run till you are out of breath and die madly! Prudence . . . how you bore me with your endless yawning!"

Philosophy is dull if it does not touch my instinct. Sweet to dream of, with the vision that adorns it, it is not science . . . or at most science in the germ. Multiple, like everything in nature, ceaselessly evolving, it is not a deduction from things, as certain solemn personages would have us believe, but rather a weapon, which we alone, even as savages, fabricate ourselves. It dares not manifest itself as a reality but as an image, even as a picture is,—admirable if the picture is a masterpiece.

Art requires philosophy, just as philosophy requires art. Otherwise, what would become of beauty?

The Colossus remounts to the pole, the world's pivot; his great mantle shelters and warms the two germs, Seraphitus, Seraphita, fertile souls, ceaselessly uniting, who issue from their boreal mists to traverse the whole universe, teaching, loving, creating.

You wish to teach me what is within myself? Learn first what is within you. You have solved the problem, I could not solve it for you. It is the task of all of us to solve it.

Toil endlessly. Otherwise, what would life be worth?

We are what we have been from the beginning; and we are what we shall be always, ships tossed about by every wind.

Shrewd, far-sighted sailors avoid dangers to which others succumb, partly, however, thanks to an indefinable something that permits one to live under the same circumstances in which another, acting in the same manner, would die.

The few use their wills, the rest resign themselves without a struggle.

*

*   *

I believe that life has no meaning unless one lives it with a will, at least to the limit of one's will. Virtue, good, evil are nothing but words, unless one takes them apart in order to build something with them; they do not win their true meaning until one knows how to apply them. To surrender oneself to the hands of one's Creator is to annul oneself and to die.

Saint Augustine and Fortunatus the Manichæan, face to face, are each of them right and wrong, for here nothing can be proved.

To surrender oneself either to the power of good or to the power of evil is a dangerous and far from creditable business. It is the excuse. . .

No one is good; no one is evil; everyone is both, in the same way and in different ways. It would be needless to point this out if the unscrupulous were not always saying the opposite.

It is so small a thing, the life of a man, and yet there is time to do great things, fragments of the common task.

I wish to love, and I cannot.

I wish not to love, and I cannot.

You drag your double along with you, and yet the two contrive to get on together.

I have been good sometimes; I do not congratulate myself because of it. I have been evil often; I do not repent it.

A sceptic, I look at all these saints, but to me they are not alive. In the niches of a cathedral they have meaning,—there only. The gargoyles, too, unforgettable monsters. My eye is not terrified by these childish grotesqueries.

The graceful ogive lightens the heaviness of the structure; the wide steps invite the curious passer-by to investigate the interior. The belfry— the cross above—the great transept—the cross within. In his pulpit the priest babbles about Hell; in their seats these ladies talk about the fashions. I like this better.

As you see, everything is serious and ridiculous also. Some weep, others laugh. The feudal castle, the thatched cottage, the cathedral, the brothel.

What is one to do about it?

Nothing.

All this must be; and, after all, it's of no consequence. The earth still turns round; everyone defecates; only Zola bothers about it.

*
*   *

These nymphs, I want to perpetuate them, with their golden skins, their searching animal odour, their tropical savours. They are here what they are everywhere, have always been, will always be. That adorable Mallarmé immortalized them, gay, with their vigilant love of life and the flesh, beside the ivy of Ville-d'Avray that entwines the oaks of Corot.

Pictures and writings are portraits of their authors. The mind must have an eye only for the work. When it looks at the public, the work collapses.

When a man says to me, "You must," I rebel.

When nature (my nature) says the same thing to me, I yield, knowing that I am beaten.

You say, "Spend yourself, spend yourself again!" It is of no value unless you suffer.

With my own understanding, I have tried to build up a superior understanding that will, if he desires it, become that of my neighbour.

The struggle is cruel, but it is not vain. It springs from pride and not from vanity.

On an azure ground a seigniorial coronet, a coronet of nettles, and as a device: "Nothing stings me."

It is a small thing but there is pride in it. Laughing, you climb your Calvary; your legs stagger under the weight of the cross; reaching the top, you grit your teeth—and then, smiling again, you avenge yourself. Spend yourself again! Woman, what have we in common?—The children!!! They are my disciples, those of the second Renaissance.

Atone for the sins of others when they are swine? Immolate yourself for these? You do not immolate yourself, you invite defeat.

Civilized! You are proud of not eating human flesh? On a raft you would eat it . . . before God, invoking Him even as you trembled.

To make up for it, you eat the heart of your neighbour every day.

Content yourself with saying, therefore, "I have not done it," since you cannot say with certainty, "I will never do it."

But all this is very gloomy? Yes, if you do not know how to laugh at it.

With an Indian undergoing torture, the pride of being able to smile in the face of pain largely compensates for the suffering. And . . . why fabricate tears in order to shed them?

One reasons, but one is free of it.

It is perhaps in this that the strength of the common people lies.

In the child, too, instinct rules reason.

*

*   *

Jean Jacques Rousseau confesses himself. It is less a need than an idea. The man of the people is dirty but quick to cleanse himself. People did not want to believe this, but they were forced to believe it. It is something quite different that Voltaire says to the nobility: "You are ridiculous, we are ridiculous, let us remain ridiculous. Candide is a naïve child; there have to be such people. . . . Let us remain what we are."

Jacques the fatalist is fated to remain the servant.

Jean Jacques Rousseau, that's another matter.

The education of Emile!! It revolts any number of good people. It remains the most difficult undertaking a man has ever attempted. I myself, in my own country, dare not think of it. Here, enlightened at last, I regard it quite calmly. I have seen a native chief who, had it not been for the French domination, would have been king, ask a white colonist, married to a white woman, for one of his children. For the right to adopt it, he was willing to give the father in payment almost all his lands and five hundred piastres which he had saved.

Here, for everyone, children are the greatest boon of nature, and everyone wants to adopt them. Such is the savagery of the Maoris, which I have chosen. All my doubts are dispelled. This sort of savage I am and will remain.

Christianity here is without understanding. . . . Happily, in spite of all its efforts, conjoined with the civilized laws of succession, marriage is only a sham ceremony. The bastard, the child of adultery remain, as in the past, monsters that exist only in the fancy of our civilization.

Here the education of Emile takes place in the broad enlightening sunshine, deliberately adopted by some and accepted by the whole of society. Smiling and free, the young girls can give birth to as many Emiles as they wish.

*

*   *

The subterfuges of language, the artifices of style, brilliant turns of the phrase that sometimes please me as an artist are not suited to my barbaric heart, which is so hard, so loving. One understands them and tries one's hand at them; it is a luxury which harmonizes with civilization and which for its beauties I do not disdain.

Let us learn to employ it and rejoice in it boldly, the sweet music which at times I love to hear—till the moment when my heart asks for silence again.

There are savages who clothe themselves now and then.

*

*   *

I am afraid that the younger generation, all coming out of the same mould—too pretty a mould, in my opinion—will never be able to efface the stamp of it.

Art for Art's sake   Why not?
Art for Life's sake   "   "
Art for Pleasure's sake   "   "
What does it matter, as long as it is art?

The artist at ten, at twenty, at a hundred is always the artist, little, middle-sized, great. Has he not his hours, his moments? Never impeccable, being a man and living. One critic says to him, "There is the North." Another says to him, "The North is the South." They blow on the artist as if he were a weathercock.

The artist dies; the heirs fall upon his work; everything is divided up: copyrights, auctions, and all the rest of it. There he is, completely stripped.

With this in mind, I strip myself beforehand. That is a comfort.

*

*   *

Cézanne paints a brilliant landscape: ultramarine background, heavy greens, glistening ochres; a row of trees, their branches interlaced, allowing, however, a glimpse of the house of his friend Zola, with its vermilion shutters turned orange by the yellow reflected from the walls. The burst of emerald greens expresses the delicate verdure of the garden, while in contrast the deep note of the purple nettles in the foreground orchestrates the simple poem. It is at Médan.

A pretentious passer-by takes an astonished glance at what he thinks is some amateur's pitiful mess and, smiling like a professor, says to Cézanne, "You paint?"

"Certainly, but not very much." . . .

"Oh, I can see that. Look here, I'm an old pupil of Corot's; and if you'll allow me, I can put all that in its proper place for you with a few skilful touches. Values, values . . . that's the whole thing!"

And the vandal impudently spreads his imbecilities over the brilliant canvas. Dirty greys cover the Oriental silks.

"How happy you must be, Monsieur!" cries Cézanne. "When you do a portrait I have no doubt you put the shine on the end of the nose just as you do on the legs of the chair."

Cézanne seizes his palette, and with his knife scrapes off all Monsieur's dirty mud. Then, after a moment of silence, he lets a tremendous_____ and, turning to Monsieur, says, "Oh!!! what a relief!"

*
*   *

My good uncle in Orleans, whom they called Zizi, because his name was Isidore and he was very small, used to tell me about the time when I came back from Peru and lived in my grandfather's house; I was seven years old.

Now and again they used to see me in the big garden stamping and flinging the sand all about me.

"Well, little Paul, what's the matter with you?" And I stamped all the harder, saying, "Baby is naughty!"

As a child I was already judging myself and feeling the need of making it known. On another occasion they found me, motionless, in silent ecstasy under a nut-tree which, side by side with a fig-tree, adorned the corner of the garden.

"What are you doing there, little Paul?"

"I am waiting for the nuts that will fall." At that time I was beginning to speak French, and I suppose, because I was in the habit of speaking Spanish, I pronounced all the letters with what seemed like affectation.

114

A little later I was whittling one day with a knife, carving dagger-handles without the dagger, all sorts of little fancies incomprehensible to grown people. A good old woman who was a friend of ours exclaimed in admiration, "He's going to be a great sculptor!" Unfortunately, this woman was no prophet.

They sent me as a day-pupil to a school in Orleans. The master said, "That child will be either an idiot or a man of genius." I have become neither the one nor the other.

One day I came home with some coloured glass marbles. My mother was angry and asked me where I had got these marbles. I hung my head and said I had traded my rubber ball for them.

"What! you, my son, *trading!*"

This word "trade" in my mother's mind meant something shameful. Poor mother! She was wrong and she was right, in this sense, that already as a child I had divined that there are many things that are not sold.

At eleven I entered the primary school where I made very rapid progress.

I notice in the *Mercure* the views of several writers on this primary school education of which they had to rid themselves later.

I will not say, as Henri de Régnier does, that this education counted for nothing in my intellectual development; on the contrary, I think it did me a great deal of good.

Besides, I believe it was there I learned, from my earliest youth, to hate hypocrisy, sham virtue, tale-bearing (*semper tres!*) and to distrust everything that was contrary to my instincts, my heart and my reason. I learned there also a little of the spirit of Escobar, a force that is very far indeed from being negligible in the struggle. There I formed the habit of concentrating on myself, ceaselessly watching what my teachers were up to, making my own playthings, and my own griefs as well, with all the responsibilities they bring with them.

But mine was a special case; in general I think the experiment is dangerous.

*

*　　　　*

Some time ago, a young man named M. Rouart gave a lecture in Belgium. I like it when well-intentioned young people, however mistaken they may be, are looking for good things and express their opinions.

His speech was eloquent, though it proved nothing; his point was that the intellectual life of one artist or another is entirely determined by the different necessities that exist in each period.

If I believed that speeches were of any use in these matters, I should give a lecture addressed to those who are not artists, telling them to "support the artists."

But by what right can you say to your neighbour, "Support me?" You must resign yourself to the fact that some will be rich and some poor. For more than thirty years I have been watching the efforts of all sorts of groups and societies and I have never seen anything that counted but individual effort.

At the Universal Exposition of 1889, the men at the head of the Beaux-Arts often went for a drink over to the café opposite, the Café Volpini. At my instigation the walls of this café had been decorated with pictures by a little group of which I was one.

It was there that Meissonier, greatest of painters, struck his forehead and said: "Gentlemen, it is high time for painters to become free and liberal. Let us throw off this mean little box of ours with its juries, its medals, its prizes—just like a school. From now on, no more medals, now that we have them all. We must enlarge the centre of our clientele and, in order to do this, make ample room for foreign artists. The dollars will come our way."

It was a splendid society. Norway, Sweden, America: the Paulsens, the Henrysens, the Harrisons, all the mediocrities, in short. A true invasion, impressionist, synthetist, liberalist, symbolist. Liberty, Equality, Fraternity. Every man to his own ism. You would have said it was a Renaissance.

The Puvis de Chavannes, the Carrières, the Cazins, and a few others, joining hands with the Caroluses, the Besnards, the Frapparts!! All the societies together cried, "Make way for the young! . . . But no more medals for them!"

It was very clever, and the receipts were enormous. . . .

M. Rouart, if I understand him, is troubled about one thing which, in spite of himself, emerges from his lecture. That is the defence of the bourgeoisie. Why is he interested in this?

Does Drumont defend Catholicism by attacking the Jews?

You see, I believe we are all workmen. Some waste themselves, others live exaltedly. We all have before us the hammer and the anvil. It is for us to create.

*

*   *

116

A symposium on the German influence.

There are many replies which I read with interest; then all at once I begin to laugh. Brunetière!

What! The *Mercure* has dared to address, to interrogate the *Revue des Deux Mondes!*

Brunetière takes so long to reflect that he does not yet know to whom he ought to apply to have his statue made.

Rodin, *perhaps!!* But his Balzac was so unsuccessful, and his Bourgeois de Calais so . . . uncouth.

And he says, "Everybody nowadays talks about everything without having learned."

Poor Rodin and Bartholomé, who thought they had learned sculpture!

Poor Remy de Gourmont, who thought he had learned something about literature! And we, the poor public, who thought there were other artists besides M. Brunetière! It is plain that the crowd bows down before the man who has charge of the relics, but, if I may believe the fable, sometimes the relics are too heavy and you drown.

Happily I was not questioned, for—without modesty—I who have never learned anything would have been tempted to reply that Corot and Mallarmé were good Frenchmen. In that case, I should be singularly mortified today.

I am not learned, but I believe there are people who are learned. I also believe that some day some learned man will discover the exact difference in weight between genius and talent.

It seems to me that just now the lower genius sinks, the higher talent rises.

I am going to do as M. Brunetière does. I am going to begin to reflect, and reflect so long that I shall no longer dare to hold a brush or write anything whatever. One must be prudent.

Do not give up wearing your hat or genius will fly away.

*

*   *

At my window, here at Atuana in the Marquesas, everything is growing dark. The dances are ended, the soft melodies have died away. But it is not still. In a crescendo the wind rushes through the branches, the great dance begins, the cyclone is in full swing. Olympus joins in the fray; Jupiter sends us his thunderbolts, the Titans roll down rocks; the river overflows.

The immense breadfruit trees are overthrown, the cocoanut trees bow their backs and their tops brush the earth. Everything is in flight, rocks, trees, corpses, carried down to the sea. What a passionate orgy of the wrathful gods!

The sun returns; the lofty cocoanut trees lift up their plumes again; man does likewise. The great anguish is over; joy has returned; the sea smiles like a child.

The reality of yesterday becomes a fable and one forgets it.

*
*   *

It is time to make an end of all this chatter. The reader is growing impatient and I shall close, but not without writing a little preface at the end.

I think (in another sense than Brunetière's) that nowadays people write far too much. Let us come to an understanding on this subject.

There are many, many who know how to write; that is indisputable. But very few, extremely few have any idea of what the art of writing, that very difficult art, really is.

The same thing is true in the plastic arts, yet everybody has a hand in them.

Still, it is the duty of everyone to try, to practise.

Side by side with art, pure art, there are—granted the richness of the human intelligence and all its faculties—a great many things to say, *and they must be said.*

There is my whole preface. It was not my desire to make a book that should have the very least appearance of a work of art (I should not be able to do so); but as a man who is well-informed about many of the things he has seen, read and heard all over the world, the civilized and the barbarous world, I have wished, nakedly, fearlessly, shamelessly, to write . . . all this.

It is my right. And the critics cannot prevent it, infamous as it may be.

Atuana, Marquesas, January—February, 1903.

END